WHO KILLED SANTA CLAUS?

A Play

by

TERENCE FEELY

LONDON
NEW YORK SYDNEY TORONTO HOLLYWOOD

SAMUEL FRENCH LTD, 26 SOUTHAMPTON STREET, STRAND, LONDON WC2E 7JE, or their authorized agents, issue licences to amateurs to give performances of this play on payment of a fee. **The fee must be paid and the licence obtained before a performance is given.**

Licences are issued subject to the understanding that it shall be made clear in all advertising matter that the audience will witness an amateur performance; and that the names of the authors of the plays shall be included on all announcements and on all programmes.

The royalty fee indicated below is subject to contract and subject to variation at the sole discretion of Samuel French Ltd.

Basic fee for each and every performance by amateurs in the British Isles — Code J

In theatres or halls seating 600 or more the fee will be subject to negotiation.

In territories overseas the fee quoted above may not apply. Application must be made to our local authorized agents, or if there is no such agent, to Samuel French Ltd, London.

Applications for professional productions other than repertory should be made to Creative Management Associates Ltd, 22 Grafton Street, London

Applications for repertory productions should be made to Samuel French

ISBN 0 573 01510 4

Printed in Great Britain by W & J Mackay Limited, Chatham

WHO KILLED SANTA CLAUS?

Presented by Bill Freedman and Alexander H. Cohen, Ltd by arrangement with Donald Albery, at the Piccadilly Theatre, London, on the 2nd April 1970, with the following cast of characters:

Connie Bell	Martha Henry
Jack Campbell Barnes	James Cairncross
Barbara Love	Honor Blackman
Christopher Moore	Edwin Richfield
Paul Reston	Maurice Kaufmann
Don Lewis	Frank Wylie
Ray Lacey	Noel Davies
Dave Ogden	Billy Hamon

The play directed by **Nicholas Barter**

Setting by Henry Barden

The action passes in Barbara Love's house in Chelsea

ACT ONE

Scene One	Early evening
Scene Two	Twenty minutes later
Scene Three	One minute later

ACT TWO

Scene One	Immediately following
Scene Two	One hour later

Time—the present

AUTHOR'S NOTE: Should the opening scene with the television prove too difficult to stage, it can easily be played off, in the study, with just a blue flicker to indicate that the source of the voice is a television set.

WHO KILLED SANTA CLAUS?

ACT I

SCENE 1

Barbara Love's home in Chelsea. Early evening.

The house is lavish, tasteful, modern. The front door is set in the centre of windows reaching to the roof. They can be obscured by long net curtains running on a rail at the top which follows the elegant concave curve of the windows. There is a hall out of which a spiral staircase leads up to a landing with doors leading off. From the hall a step leads down to the living-room through large sliding double doors. There is a door leading from the living-room to the study, and a large double-doored hatch through which the kitchen can be seen. A long fitment, incorporating a desk, runs the whole length of one wall, and continues under the hatch and against the adjacent wall. It is stacked with drinks under the hatch. There is an Ansaphone on the desk, and a small tape recorder stands on a table. The furniture is elegant and comfortable. There is a television built into the wall facing the audience. A picture slides down to cover it when not in use. There are Christmas cards everywhere, and a Christmas tree with lights on inside the living-room doors.

When the CURTAIN *rises, Connie and Barnes are sitting side by side with their backs to the audience watching television. Barbara is on the screen, in full close-up.*

Barbara (*on the screen*) . . . If you don't agree, children, well, that's all right. You're entitled to your own opinion. I just think there's a bit more to Christmas than opening the loot on Christmas morning. Still, maybe I'm old-fashioned. And don't forget, if you have any spare toys you know where to send them. Nobody's going to call you a hero if you do or a Scrooge if you don't—it's up to you. Happy Christmas, children, from Auntie Barbara and all of us, and I'll see you next week.

The applause of the studio audience is heard.

The camera pans to see Connie sitting at a desk piled with letters and Christmas cards in medium shot. She smiles and waves. Pan further to show camera crew. They wave. Fade and roll credits and title music. Barnes rises and switches off, then switches on the lights

Connie Well, Auntie Barbara wraps it up for another year.
Barnes Got to hand it to that girl, she's a knockout.
Connie What about me?
Barnes You looked delicious.
Connie Never mind how I looked, does that mean you've given up?
Barnes Certainly not, I've got plans.

Barbara puts her key in the door

Connie Well you'd better hurry up—I've got a few plans of my own.
Barnes You know you worry me sometimes Connie.

Barbara enters, laden with Christmas parcels

Barbara God, the crowds! Hello you two.
Barnes Here, let me.
Barbara What are you doing chatting up my secretary at this time of night, Jack? (*To Connie*) I thought you were coming shopping with me.
Connie Well I was, but . . .
Barnes My fault entirely. Gave Connie a lift with the champagne then stayed to watch the programme. Super.
Barbara Did Mrs Biggs put out the glasses in the study?
Barnes (*looking in the study*) Yes, regiments of them.
Connie And reinforcements in the dining room.
Barbara Get the mail, would you Connie, it's all over the floor.
Connie Probably all cards from people we missed out. (*She picks up the mail from the front door*)
Barbara Heavens, what a day! I wish you'd been with me in Harrods, Jack, there was this extraordinary woman shoplifting.
Barnes Shoplifting?
Barbara No—correction. She wasn't shoplifting, she was looting. And it all went under this extraordinary coat. She was slim as a rail when she came in and by the time she went out she was nine months gone. The doorman even helped her into a taxi!

Connie brings back the mail

Connie Didn't you tell someone?
Barbara Well, it is Christmas after all. (*She opens the mail*)
Connie Barbara, if it came up on the show you know you'd tell five million child viewers it was their duty to report it.
Barbara Of course I would. For children you've got to keep morality simple.
Barnes Quite right. Keep it simple, keep 'em secure. Kids hate fine distinctions.
Barbara Why do you producers always talk like telegrams?
Barnes The message gets through quicker that way.
Barbara Oh Lord, here's one from Dottie Milburn—we forgot her birthday, too.

Connie Aunties should practice what they preach.
Barbara Nonsense, what Auntie Barbara does when she's off the box is entirely her own affair.
Connie But isn't that rather dangerous? I mean what if they were to find out? Oh look—we got one of Fanny's special ones this year.
Barbara Find out what?—that I didn't report a shoplifter?
Connie Well . . . anything . . .
Barnes I must say it's a great relief to have the Christmas programme over. But next year we've *got* to do something different. We've done the stories behind the Carols for the last three years.
Barbara Well, it *is* the obvious thing.
Barnes Exactly. We forget our little masters can shoot up like hollyhocks in three years. They know an idle Auntie when they see one.
Barbara Well as long as we don't try to compete with sex for beginners on BBC.
Barnes Quite agree. At this rate they'll be committing adultery before they can spell it.

The doorbell rings

Barbara Don't bother—it'll only be more carol singers.
Connie I'd better draw the curtains or they'll be gathered round out there like dolphins round a diving bell.

Connie goes to the hall, pays the carol singers and then draws the curtains

Barnes Barbara, since I'm here. There *is* something I'd like to talk to you about before the party.
Barbara Aha! I thought you weren't here just to deliver the champagne.
Barnes We have to sign the new contract with the company straight after the holiday.
Barbara Yes—and we made a very good deal.
Barnes But what we didn't agree was a new arrangement between you and me.
Barbara Darling Jack, you never give in, do you? There's not going to be a new arrangement between you and me.
Barnes Now listen, Barbara . . .
Connie (*returning with more mail*) Oh, that'll be nice!
Barbara What's that?
Connie The GPO will cut off our telephone from midnight tonight, as requested.
Barbara Must be for next door—she's going away for the winter. Lucky devil!
Barnes Yes . . . well, I'd better be off. I have still to wrap up Jennie's Christmas present.
Barbara See you later, Jack!

Barnes kisses Barbara quickly

Barnes And I want to take a shower before the party. (*He kisses Connie* *and pats her bottom at the same time, then goes to the door)*

Connie (*smiling at Barbara*) Jack—about that shower.

Barnes Yes?

Connie Better make it a cold one.

Barnes Optimist.

Barnes exits

Connie opens more mail

Barbara Dear Jack—I think he sometimes wishes he was back in the army, with us as his platoon.

Connie Yes. He's still pretty good at the assault course. I didn't know you were kinky about tombstones. (*She hands Barbara a letter*)

Barbara What? Response to your enquiry—black marble our speciality—Dignity with Economy—Please to give you a quotation . . .

Connie What is it, a joke?

Barbara The post always goes lunatic at this time of year.

Connie Yes, but it says "Dear Miss Love".

Barbara They probably got my name from a mailing list.

Connie It's disgraceful—imagine that coming to someone who's seriously ill. They'd get an awful shock.

Barbara Well I'm not seriously ill and I won't be in shock until after the children's party tomorrow. How many are coming, by the way?

Connie Twelve—from Dr Barnardo's—ages four to eleven.

Barbara Are you sure we've got enough presents?

Connie We have now.

Barbara I mean we don't want a repetition of last year when that sweet little girl was left out—and I had to console her with a ten guinea pair of ear-rings.

Connie They're coming at three and the photographer will be here at three thirty.

Barbara I wish we could do without the photographer. It does seem a bit cynical.

Connie Jack insists. He says Good Samaritans should be seen.

Barbara He'd have left the man from Jericho lying bleeding by the roadside till the cameras arrived. Oh My God!

Connie What?

Barbara I forgot to get him a present for tonight.

Connie No you didn't—I got it yesterday.

Barbara What did you get?

Connie One of those shavers with three heads.

Barbara Very appropriate. One for each of his. And what did you get for the rest of the team?

Connie Those pens with a light on the end.

Barbara For writing dirty books in the dark?

Connie Well I'm sorry—

Barbara Oh Connie, I wasn't criticizing—you've been a very good secretary. But I suppose you'll be needing one of your own, now you've got your own little spot on the show.

Connie You really don't mind?

Barbara Why should I mind? I suggested it. Oh there's the evening paper—be a darling and get it, would you? What time are the others due?

Connie Eight o'clock they said—unless they rang to alter it.

Barbara Did you check the Ansaphone?

Connie No, I meant to, but I got involved in the programme.

Connie exits to the hall

Barbara switches on the Ansaphone

Ansaphone This is an automatic answering device. Miss Love is not at home. If you will record your message she will attend to it on her return. Please speak now.

A Yorkshire voice—Mr Lee the printer—answers

Lee's voice Oh—er—aye, yes. (*He clears his throat*) This is me, you see—Mr Lee, the printer.

Connie enters with the evening paper

It's about your new stationery, you see. Your message about the black border you want round it. I'd like to speak to you about it . . . Well, I know I'm speaking now but I mean properly, you know . . . Oh heck, I'll call back when you're yourself again.

Connie What does he mean—a black border?

Barbara Oh, you know Mr Lee—progress confuses him. I bet he thinks Jumbo jets are for washing down elephants.

Connie But there were no problems about the new writing paper—(*Takes a bill out of the evening paper*) What's this—a new economy drive?

Barbara What is it?

Connie It's the bill from the newsagent up to date and confirming you want all the papers cancelled from tonight.

Barbara Has everyone gone mad? What is it about Christmas.

The Ansaphone crackles and Dickie speaks

Dickie's voice Hello darling!

Barbara (*jumps*) Oh! That blasted thing.

Dickie's voice This is Dickie. Look, I had a preliminary chat with the company about your contract today. Must have a talk with you urgently. Give me a yell soonest will you, darling.

Barbara (*frowning*) He must have hit a snag.

Connie Just agent talk.

Barbara I don't know. They've been a bit evasive lately. Basically they resent independent outfits like ours.

Connie Oh that's just imagination. They adore you *and* the show and you know it.

Barbara Oh I suppose you're right.

Connie You're just tired. It's been a long, hard series. Anyway, we can't afford to have you crack up, can we? I'll get you a drink—and then you must write the cards for Jack's present and the others. (*She goes to fix the drink*)

Barbara looks through the parcels

Barbara Is this Jack's?

Connie No, that's the little clock for Mrs Biggs.

Barbara This?

Connie No, that's for Jane.

Barbara How about this one?

Connie That's funny. I don't remember that one.

Barbara I'm not surprised—how you can keep them all in your head . . .

Connie No it's not that . . . (*She brings the drinks over*)

Barbara Oo look, there's a little tag on it addressed to me!

Connie D'you recognize the writing?

Barbara No.

Connie I'd swear it wasn't there this morning.

Barbara It probably came this afternoon and Mrs Biggs took it in. (*She tears off the wrapping and throws it aside, disclosing a box*)

Connie Perhaps it's from an unknown admirer.

Barbara I'm all agog! (*She takes the lid off the box and stops, a little shaken*) It's a—coffin. My God, I've enslaved an undertaker! (*She takes it out of the box*)

Connie takes it from her

Connie There's a little brass plate on it. "Here lie the mortal remains of Barbara Love. Died twenty-fourth December nineteen . . ." But that's—today. Why should anyone want to send you something like that? (*She is more puzzled than frightened*)

Barbara It's obviously a joke.

Connie It's an odd idea of festive fun. (*Idly she tries the lid. It comes off. Inside is a doll*) Ugh!

Barbara What a gruesome little thing. That purple face. And what's this round its neck? It's a bit of stocking. Connie, look.

Connie I can't. It's sick. That's one of your dresses it's got on.

Barbara Well, it is a bit like it, admittedly.

Connie It's an exact copy. Don't you see what it means? That obscene—thing—has been sent to you by someone you know. Someone who's had the time to take great pains over memorizing a particular dress.

Barbara Oh Connie. It's probably some demented parent whose little Johnnie didn't win a prize in the painting competiton.

Connie How would they know about your dress?

Barbara Well, I've worn it on the box.

Connie No you haven't, Barbara, and you know it. No—it's all of a piece.

The black border round the writing paper, cancelling the papers, cutting off the telephone, that stuff about the tombstone—and now this.

Barbara Connie, you're taking it far too seriously. I've had kinks before—everyone on the box has had them.

Connie Never like this. There's something sick about this.

Barbara (*trying to jolly her*) Couldn't be much sicker than the man who wanted me to meet him under the clock at Victoria wearing nothing but thigh boots and a riding hat!

Connie smiles faintly, then drinks, and smiles again

Connie Yes, I know everyone's had the sexpots but . . .

Barbara And everyone's had the sinister ones too. Poor old Billy gets a death threat every time he reads a news item about fox-hunting. He showed me one of the letters once. It said "I'm going to come round and cut your brush off and see how you like that!"

Connie Yes, but how would they know about your dress? A stranger wouldn't know about it.

Barbara Oh Connie, you know as well as I do that once a nut gets it in for you, you become an obsession with him. He's probably read every word that's ever been published about me, followed me home from the studios, taken secret snapshots. He could have seen me in that dress anywhere. He's probably just a forty-five-year-old puberty case.

Connie Well, at least it's not heavy breathing down the telephone. I don't think I could stand that.

Barbara Poor Dodo Jackson had that for three months. She got to like it in the end. She won't look at a man now unless he's got a touch of asthma.

Connie (*laughs*) Barbara, you're a terrible liar.

Barbara Anyway, I've always got my cannon. (*She gets a gun from a drawer*)

Connie You should have given it back to the rifle club.

Barbara Ah wouldn't do that if ah was yew! (*She twirls it western-style and puts it back in the drawer*) Well, at least it'll be something to put in your diary.

Connie Yes. It's been getting a bit dull, lately. Now, we'd better write the gift cards for Jack and the boys. It'll be eight o'clock before we know it and we haven't even changed or got the drinks organized yet.

Barbara finishes her drink

Now then there's Jack's, and those are the others. (*She hands two parcels to Barbara*)

Barbara Now the annual problem—how to compose the right little messages in order of seniority.

Connie How about this—"To Darling Jack—the Tottenham Hotspur".

Barbara He supports Fulham doesn't he, the masochist?

Connie Don't get technical.

Barbara We could call Ray "The Adult most likely to Consent". Are you sure there's nothing from the boys on the Ansaphone?

Connie I don't know—we switched off after Dickie's message.

Barbara Let's see. (*She switches on the Ansaphone*)

There is a pause. The voice which now speaks is bizarre, disguised, electronically distorted

Voice Miss Love? Miss Barbara Love? Are you sitting quietly? Then I'll begin. You won't know my voice, Miss Love, but you will, I think, know my name. My name—at least so far as you are concerned, Miss Love—is Death. Did you like my little present? Just a pale imitation I'm afraid. But I'm coming to your party tonight. I'll bring you the real thing then. That's how you'll look, Miss Love. Good-bye for now.

The two women stand transfixed. Then Barbara lunges for the telephone. She starts to dial

CURTAIN

SCENE 2

The same. Twenty minutes later.

When the CURTAIN *rises, Connie is ushering in Superintendent Moore. Barbara is standing nervously in the room. Both girls have changed. The Superintendent is elegant down to his slim, mirror-like shoes. He has the manner of an Oxford don of independent means*

Connie Barbara, this is Superintendent Moore from the Chelsea Police station.

Moore Miss Love—how nice to see you. I've often admired you on the television. Such poise. (*Admiring a china figure*) Oh, isn't that a Donnini? Charming! One can always spot him by his reds. He used a secret vegetable dye, you know, and a special method of firing. I thought I'd come to see you myself when I heard what your problem was. You don't want a lot of chaps in blue grinding about. Good chaps, mind you, but they tend to fill a room up from wall to wall. They take all the oxygen. D'you mind if I sit down?

Barbara (*a bit dazed*) No, I'm so sorry—please do.

Moore sits down. As he does so he catches sight of the doll where Connie has thrown it. He reaches out a long arm and picks it up

Moore Thank you. That's the little lassie, is it? Reminds me of Grutmann's work in Vienna.

Barbara Grutmann? Was he a . . . ?

Moore He was a doll maker. Exquisite sense of form and balance. Some of his faces would break your heart.

Connie (*tactfully*) Have you—er—been with the police long, Superintendent?

Moore I joined them from Military Intelligence after the war. Got tired of spies, you know. Dreary, grey little people, always lying. No, for real colour give me your common criminal every time. That's where I met Grutmann and his dolls. We used them during the war. They used to blow up when you lifted their skirts. Very nasty mind, Mr Grutmann. (*He lifts the doll's skirt*) These are pretty. Chinese silk. (*He shows the doll's underwear to Barbara*) Do you have any like these, Miss Love?

Barbara (*looking and turning away*) No.

Moore Forgive my asking, but it might have been significant.

Barbara How?

Moore I understand the dress is a detailed copy of one of your own.

Barbara An exact miniature.

Moore Which argues a certain acquaintance with you.

Connie That's what I said.

Moore If the underwear had shown the same accuracy of detail, it would—I imagine—have considerably narrowed the field.

Connie gives a short delighted yelp of laughter then shuts up hastily

Barbara Yes—I see.

Moore Of course, the fact that these charming little knickers are not accurate cannot be taken as proof of the reverse, however. That the prankster is not an intimate acquaintance. A man of subtlety would have spotted the trap and avoided it.

Barbara Yes—yes, of course.

Moore looks at her quizzically

What am I supposed to say now?

Moore (*putting the doll by the Ansaphone*) It is not incumbent upon you to say anything, Miss Love. Of course, if there had been a recently fractured sexual relationship it would have been a direction in which to look.

Barbara exchanges a look with Connie

Barbara No. There is—nothing—like that.

Moore has not missed the exchange of glances. He changes gear, a tactic he will use frequently

Moore Any professional enemies?

Barbara No—I don't think so. But then one doesn't always know one's enemies.

Moore Very true—they can be almost as deceitful as one's friends. Now, tell me about your programme.

Barbara My programme?

Moore Yes, I find in a case like this, I'm investigating not so much a mystery—more a way of life.

Barbara Well, it's a package show. It was one of the first.

Moore A package show?

Barbara Yes. The company gives us the money and we deliver the show. Jack Campbell-Barnes and I started it together. We own half each.

Moore (*looking around the room*) It must be very lucrative.

Connie It is.
Moore And who is the fortunate Mr Campbell-Barnes?
Connie He's the producer, he'll be coming tonight.
Moore What's he like?
Connie Ex-Major—dominant, energetic—you know, tower-of-strength type.
Barbara His wife's an invalid. He's got that sort of maternal thing men like that get.
Connie I must say I'd never thought of Jack as the great earth Mother!
Barbara I don't mean he's soft or anything. Far from it. He's a survivor.
Moore D'you know, I always find that one of those curiously loaded expressions.
Connie Yes, so do I.
Barbara Oh I don't mean it in any critical way. It's just that he went through a bad patch once and came out the other side.
Moore What kind of bad patch?
Barbara It was some kind of enquiry into corruption at the BBC.
Moore Not corruption at the BBC!
Connie You've shocked him!
Moore Well, it *is* rather like finding your bank manager cheating at Crockford's.
Connie Jack was cleared, of course.
Barbara Yes, I was going to make that clear.

There is another moment between Connie and Barbara

Moore And who else is coming?
Barbara Well, the rest of my little family, really. There's Paul Reston, he's the director of my show.
Moore What sort of man is he?
Connie Very good at his job, rather prickly. Used to be in the British fencing team.
Barbara Oh did he—I didn't know that.
Connie No?
Barbara No. He's dark and neurotic—possessive in the sort of way a lot of women like.
Connie Oh come on, Barbara—he's not Bluebeard.
Barbara Well, I'd say at least five o'clock shadow.
Connie He's just a bit intense, that's all.
Barbara A bit intense! What about the time he smashed three monitors in the Control Room?
Moore That's very spectacular. Why on earth should he do that?
Connie They went wrong. Paul's a television perfectionist.
Moore He must get through a lot of monitors. Is he married?
Barbara Divorced. His wife was one of those thin bright model girls. She looked like a neon light in a wig.
Connie He's the sort of man who attracts bitches.

A look passes between Connie and Barbara

Moore Well, that's very comprehensive. From that description I should recognize him on sight. Who else is coming?
Barbara Well, there's Don Lewis—he writes the show.
Moore What's he like?
Barbara I always think of him as a ravaged Peter Pan.
Connie Lives with a black girl out of "Hair".
Barbara A sort of trendy Wendy.
Connie He loves gin and fast cars.
Moore Well, there'a a volatile mixture.
Barbara He had a bad scare a couple of years ago. He was drunk and thought he'd hit a woman. He hadn't but it chastened him.
Connie He's also got a very sharp tongue. When he and Ray get together, it's cat and dog.
Moore Ray being?
Connie Ray Lacey, the make-up man. He's very clever.
Barbara Queer as a cloth hammer and doesn't care who knows it. He's great fun.
Connie He got a medal once for diving into a rough sea after a child.
Barbara Insists he only did it to shrink his new jeans.
Connie He was a child actor. Then a dancer. And he was in a monastery for a time.
Moore Why did he leave?
Barbara Oh, he'll never be serious about that. Just says he wanted to get out of the habit.
Connie D'you remember that time he made a pass at Paul? It was hilarious.
Barbara Oh nonsense, Connie, he didn't make a pass. It was just a bit of fun.
Connie Paul didn't think so.
Barbara Paul just wasn't in the mood.
Connie That's what Ray thought. He thought that . . .
Barbara Connie, stop it—I think you're being unfair to both of them.
Connie It was only a joke.

There is a silence. Moore absorbs it

Moore Anyone else?
Barbara No, that's everyone.
Moore And they're all good friends . . .
Barbara Yes.

Moore looks at her for a moment then briskly changes tack again

Moore Well now, perhaps we'd better hear our prankster's little Christmas message. (*He knows this will drive Barbara out, which is what he wants*)
Barbara I'd rather not hear it again, if you don't mind.
Moore Of course.

Barbara exits through the main sliding doors

Connie makes to follow her

If you don't mind, Miss Bell—machines are something of a mystery to me.

Connie switches on the Ansaphone, and begins to wind back

Connie It's quite simple.
Moore Unlike my trade, Miss Bell, which is singularly complicated.
Connie Oh? It's ready now. (*She puts the doll in the desk drawer*)
Moore My job, you see, is helping people. But the people I help make me feel, on the whole, more like the Marquis de Sade.
Connie Perhaps you're too sensitive.
Moore Oh I am! D'you know, I felt quite shy on meeting Miss Love.
Connie Nobody would have guessed.
Moore She's a most attractive woman. One hadn't quite expected that superb colouring.
Connie You should get a new aerial. Shall I play it now?
Moore She must have many admirers.
Connie Five million, between the ages of three and twelve.
Moore You are agile, Miss Bell.
Connie You are devious, Superintendent.
Moore You have no idea how devious.
Connie Oh but I have. My chess teacher warned me about people like you.
Moore And what sort of people are they?
Connie Oh, the sort that if they want to know the time, they ask you if you've lost your watch.
Moore Was he a good chess teacher?
Connie I thought so. He taught me always to guard my queen.
Moore In some games that's a sure way to lose her.

Connie's evasiveness has told Moore all he wants to know—there is an affair somewhere. Connie looks disconcerted

Shall we hear it now?

Connie switches on the tape

Voice Miss Love? Miss Barbara Love? Are you sitting quietly? Then I'll begin. You won't know my voice, Miss Love, but you will, I think, know my name. My name—at least so far as you are concerned, Miss Love—is Death. Did you like my little present? Just a pale imitation, I'm afraid. But I'm coming to your party tonight. I'll bring you the real thing then. That's how you'll look, Miss Love. Good-bye for now.
Moore Mmm—it'll never get in the charts, will it? Neither of you recognize anything about the voice, I suppose?
Connie No it's obviously been squeezed.

Moore looks a question

Moore Squeezed?
Connie Electronically distorted.
Moore Is that the sort of thing one learns in television?
Connie Yes, but you don't have to be in TV to know how to do it.

Moore Oh dear, I thought I had a clue.

Barbara enters

Barbara Have you heard it?
Moore Yes.
Barbara What did you think?
Moore It's been "squeezed" of course—but that's not the point. There are certain things which can't be disguised—rhythms, patterns, intonations.
Barbara For instance?
Moore For instance, in that one short speech our man used four questions —"Miss Love? Miss Barbara Love? Are you sitting quietly?" and "Did you like my little present?" Now do we know anyone with that habit of speech?
Barbara No—no I don't think so. But it's not the kind of thing that strikes one.
Moore Unless one is looking for it. Well, we must all start looking.
Barbara But I must know hundreds of people.
Moore They are not all coming to your party tonight.
Barbara You surely don't think he'll come?

Moore widens his eyes and nods

Moore Yes, I do.
Connie But if he really intends to come tonight, why should he give us advance warning?
Moore We're dealing with a perverse mind. If he says he's coming to the party I think we should believe him.
Barbara But he must know I'd call the police.
Connie He can't break in without us knowing.
Barbara And he's hardly likely to come to the front door and ring the bell.
Moore I believe that is precisely what he will do.

Connie gets the point

Barbara Then you can pick him up instantly.
Moore And how will I know who he is?
Barbara Well it's obvious—he'll be the one who hasn't been invited.
Moore On the contrary.
Barbara (*dawning*) What!
Moore I believe our prankster is one of your guests.

There is a silence, broken by the doorbell ringing

Connie I'll go.
Moore I suggest you say nothing about my being a policeman. I find it throws a damper on a party. They'll all start talking about parking in the West End.
Barbara Then who shall we say you are?
Moore (*beaming*) An old friend from Hampshire.

Connie exits to the hall

Barbara But what's your name? Your Christian name?
Moore I have five, but you may call me Christopher.
Barbara (*shaking hands*) All right—Christopher.

Connie enters with Paul Reston, director of Barbara's show. He is dark, tense, neurotic, but attractive to women. He is instantly conscious of Moore

Paul darling!
Reston Barbara! Merry Christmas!

Reston and Barbara kiss on the cheek. He tries to hold her for a moment, longer than one would expect. She pulls away gently. Connie turns to Moore

Connie And this is . . .
Barbara (*quickly*) Christopher Moore—an old friend of mine from Hampshire, and this is Paul Reston, the director of my show.
Reston, **Moore** } D'you do . . .

Reston seems a little hostile to and suspicious of Moore. He looks at Barbara

Moore I was just about to compliment your leading lady on what chemistry she has with the camera. It's a face made to be televised.
Barbara Thank you, kind sir.
Moore No, I mean it. It's something to do with the mouth and the gleaming hair and the way the light just catches the eyes. There you see, there's a flash of it when you moved your head. And there! You see! Another flash as you moved your head. Fascinating, isn't it?
Barbara I feel like a lighthouse.
Reston Whereabouts in Hampshire?
Moore Oh—little place called Beaulieu, actually.
Reston Ah yes—I know some people in Beaulieu, the Russells. D'you know them?
Moore Yes, they're friends of the Jolliffes—funny, I've never heard them mention you.
Reston (*irritated, the tables have been turned*) No, you wouldn't—they're only slight acquaintances. Where d'you know Barbara from?
Moore Oh, it's a long story.
Reston I've got time.
Barbara Heavens, what is this—an interrogation? Have a drink.

Connie goes to the bar

Reston (*spiky*) You must forgive me. I'm always fascinated by Barbara's "old friends". She seems to have so many of them.
Barbara Oh Paul, come on. You make me sound like a Benevolent Society.
Reston But you are, my darling—you spread benevolence quite—promiscuously.
Connie (*hastily*) Whisky?

Moore Glenfiddich! What cultured girls you are.

Connie pours out the drink

Connie You won't want water.
Moore My regard for you mounts by the minute.
Barbara Paul?
Reston (*putting Moore down*) The usual. Cooking Scotch and soda.
Connie Have you seen any of the others, Paul? (*She hands out the drinks*)
Reston Saw Jack earlier. He said he might be a bit late.
Barbara Yes, I know!
Reston Are you in our business, Mr Moore?
Moore No, I'm an anthropologist.
Reston Oh, you mean darkest Africa and all that?
Moore Not really. I confine most of my observations to the King's Road, Chelsea and Knightsbridge. I call it my Kensington Congo.

Connie exits to the study

Reston Are you happy in your work?
Moore I find it agreeable.
Reston An anthropologist's a sort of professional voyeur, isn't he?
Moore Yes—I believe television caters for the amateur.
Reston Still, you must feel like a little tin god looking down on us poor mortals.
Moore Not really. It's rather rewarding observing one's own failings in others.
Reston Oh, you do have failings then?
Moore Oh, troops of them. Chief of which for instance, is my nature. It's so amiable that it's almost impossible to arouse me.
Reston No-one is so burnt-out that he can't be re-ignited.
Moore Oh you'd need big bellows for my embers, Mr Reston. Barbara could manage it, of course.
Reston I've no doubt about that—proper little fire-raiser our Barbara, aren't you my darling? (*He tries to cuddle her, but she breaks away*)
Barbara I don't know whether that's a compliment or not.
Reston Of course she can be cold, too—the original fire and ice girl. Somebody should patent her—heater and fridge in one glossy package.
Barbara (*starting to hit back*) The trouble with heaters is that they don't work unless you know how to switch them on.
Reston Yes and sometimes they go out again even then.
Barbara Yes, sad, isn't it? Still, we can't always have everything our own way.
Reston Some of us think we can. Some of us think we can own everyone, pick them up and put them down as it pleases us.
Barbara And some of us are more easily put down than others.
Reston How marvellous to be so sure of oneself! Still, I suppose once people have become just objects, it's easy.
Barbara Some people are just objects.

The doorbell rings

Connie enters from the study

Connie Shall I?
Barbara Yes—I'll finish off in there.

Connie exits to the hall.
Barbara exits to the study. Reston stands fuming for a second then follows her, slamming the door behind him

Moore moves to the study door, then away again as—

Barnes enters, followed after a brief moment by Connie

Barnes All alone, are you? Left you holding the fort, have they?
Moore Christopher Moore.
Barnes Yes, Connie told me. Jack Campbell Barnes. You're an anthropologist, are you?
Moore Yes. And you are a producer for the television.
Connie He's the best.
Barnes You'll go a long way my girl. Here, handle that with extreme care—it might explode—gorgonzola. If you weren't so valuable to Barbara I'd steal you away for my own secretary. Wouldn't I be right, Moore?
Connie Flatterer! You're only saying that because it's true.
Moore Were you ever an interviewer?
Barnes Yes, I was as a matter of fact. How d'you know?
Moore You have an interrogatory style.
Barnes You should have seen me in action old man. Sweet as pie in rehearsal, then carve them up the minute we get on camera.
Connie He loves to pretend he's an ogre. Take no notice. (*To Barnes*) Behave yourself and have a drink.
Barnes Have you got—

Connie is already holding up the Glenfiddich

You remembered!
Connie Naturally.
Barnes Give me a girl who forgets your birthday but remembers your drink.
Moore So, it's your palate I have to thank, Mr Barnes.
Barnes You're an addict too, are you?
Moore Oh, beyond hope. If Scotland had given us nothing but whisky and the kilt she would still have warmed our hearts and cooled our ambitions.
Barnes I'll drink to that.
Connie (*to Moore*) Don't encourage him too much, he's got to watch his liver. Must be like an old cavalry saddle by now.
Barnes Nonsense girl! I've got the liver of a man half my age.
Connie Well if he's got yours, he's in trouble.
Moore Now Paul Reston is the director of the show and you're the . . .?
Barnes Producer—for my sins.

Moore Yes, producing must be something of a worry.
Connie That's how he got those sexy grey whiskers.
Moore Less of a worry of course if you've got a happy ship.
Barnes We're just a big happy family, my chaps.

There are sounds of a row in the study

Moore Disputes, of course, occur in the best regulated families.
Barnes (*trying to drown the noise*) Yes, we have discussions you know. But there's a difference between a discussion and a row.
Moore Yes. A row is a discussion one's just beginning to lose isn't it? As someone is beginning to lose that one in there.
Connie Oh, that doesn't mean anything. It's just their way of communicating.
Moore By megaphone, I presume.

Connie exchanges a glance with Barnes

Connie I'd better break them up or they'll be talking shop in there all night.

Connie exits to the study

Barnes Very efficient young woman, our Connie.
Moore You set great store by her.
Barnes I do indeed, old man—I admire efficiency.
Moore I seem to have seen her on the television, too.
Barnes You have. I gave her a bit to do on the show.
Moore I seem to remember her as being rather good.
Barnes She is. She's damn good!
Moore Worth a bigger part I would have thought.
Barnes No question! But you have to tread very warily, you know.
Moore Oh?
Barnes I have my leading lady to consider.
Moore Ah!
Barnes Did hint at it once to Barbara . . .
Moore Not well received?
Barnes No, she's come as far as she's going to come giving Connie what she's got now.
Moore Barbara tells me you own half the show. Doesn't that give you a little leverage?
Barnes Half is a very approximate figure, old man. It's actually forty-nine per cent.
Moore How very frustrating.
Barnes Yes. It's like being the look-out at an orgy. You have all the responsibility and none of the pleasure.
Moore Yes. A clever girl, is Barbara.
Barnes She writes a better contract than any six lawyers. She's got us all tied down. But does it with such charm that you can't resent it.
Moore Not ever?
Barnes Well, she can get a bit possessive sometimes. Like one year we tried

bringing wives and girl friends and what have you to this do. It was not a success.

Moore Just as your Connie idea was not a success.

Barnes Oh, Connie doesn't know I even tried.

Moore No, of course not.

Barnes Well, she doesn't know it from me, old man, I can assure you. My relationship with the girl is purely professional—purely professional.

The doorbell rings

Connie, Barbara and Reston enter from the study. Connie goes to the hall

Barbara Jack darling—Happy Christmas.

Moore Have you two heating experts made it up?

Reston and Barbara look startled and embarrassed

Reston Why don't you mind your own business?

Barbara No, I'm afraid Paul blew a fuse. He thinks I'm a little hard on some of the guests in the show.

Connie enters with Donald Lewis. Lewis is a ravaged Peter Pan. The cast of his face is young despite the lines and clefts in it. His manner is shy and slightly sinister. He gives Barbara a present

Barbara Donald! Oh thank you.

Lewis Hello Barbara—Jack—Paul.

Lewis and Barbara kiss desultorily on the cheek

Barbara How's my favourite TV writer?

Lewis Written out. How's my favourite TV star?

Barbara Worn out. Merry Christmas and have a drink.

Lewis Gin and tonic please.

Barnes That's no drink for a Scotsman.

Connie pours a drink for Lewis

Lewis I'm not a Scotsman—I'm a Glaswegian.

Barbara Oh, I'm so sorry—you haven't met. This is Christopher Moore, an old friend of mine. This is Donald Lewis, the writer on the show.

Moore Ah yes—the one with the girlfriend in "Hair".

Lewis Thank you for that anyway—Paul usually calls her my hairy girl-friend.

Reston I love her—every little follicle.

Lewis By the way, she says her friends have laid on a happening for me. I must be back by midnight.

Connie hands Lewis his drink

Barbara Oh come on, Cinderella, you know it'll only be another Watch-night Service in the nude. Take your drink.

Moore A vital member of the team, Mr Lewis!
Lewis (*taking his drink*) Well, somebody's got to write the words.
Barnes Oh come on, less of the modesty, man! He's a wizard with words. You've got to be to keep children interested.
Lewis Not at all. The only trick is not to write down to them.
Moore Still, it must be rather restricting.
Lewis In what way?
Moore Well, staying away from subjects that might distress or frighten them, for instance.
Lewis Don't you believe it. Children are tougher nuts than most people imagine. They have a positive relish for the sinister.
Barbara It's true—children don't frighten easily. We had a letter in from a little boy last week who said why didn't we put the show on after his parents had gone to bed and really get down to it.
Barnes (*indicating Lewis*) Mind you, if anyone could scare 'em, this fellow could. I remember that novel of yours—the thriller. Most horrific thing I've ever read. Did you ever read it, Barbara?
Barbara Yes, I believe I did. (*She looks speculatively at Lewis. She is suddenly upset*) I must go and see about the champagne.
Connie I'll come and help.

Barbara and Connie exit to the kitchen, through the main doors, closing them

Moore Have you written many thrillers, Mr Lewis?

Reston goes to the bar

Lewis No, that's the only one. No time.
Moore Oh?
Lewis A series like Barbara's, one every week—it's insatiable. You've no sooner finished one than you're on to the next. It eats you up.
Barnes Yes, but it pays well for its grub, old man.
Lewis Oh I'm not denying that.
Moore Perhaps Mr Lewis means that man cannot live by cake alone.

Lewis responds to Moore's prompting

Lewis It's just that I've done four years' hard already. I've got another two to do on my present contract. By the time I get round to it the new book may have gone bad.
Moore Are there no such things as sabbaticals in the television?
Lewis I have spoken to Mr Producer sir about that.
Barnes Now, Don, you know it's not my fault. I'd have given you six months off. I'd have released you from your contract, even.
Moore There speaks an enlightened producer!
Lewis (*to Moore*) Yes, but it hasn't happened yet, has it?
Barnes It's Barbara—she values you so highly. She relies on you.
Lewis Barbara! It's always—I think I'll have another.

Lewis goes to the bar. Reston turns to him

Reston Here, let me. (*He sloshes gin into Lewis's glass, followed by tonic*) Mr Moore is an anthropologist. That used to be your field, didn't it?

Lewis Not really my field, no. I wrote a documentary on Margaret Mead once, that's all. Learned quite a lot about it.

Reston Still—you should have a lot to talk about.

Moore Not really. Miss Mead adorns a totally different area of the science.

Reston Oh yes, I forgot. Mr Moore operates in the Harrods belt.

Lewis What, in anthropology?

Moore Don't be deceived into thinking that the only jungles left are in Africa. Primitive tribal law still holds sway in Montpelier Square . . .

The doorbell rings

Connie passes along the hall from the kitchen

Connie I'll get it. It'll be Ray.

Moore Ray?

Barnes Ray Lacey. He's our make-up man. Best there is.

Lewis Does most of his work on himself.

Barnes Oh come on now, Donald—it's Christmas.

Connie enters with Ray Lacey. Lacey is unashamedly camp both in dress and manner. He has extremely long eyelashes

Lacey Hello darlings, sorry I'm late! I dropped my lipstick! Just as Gordon Honeycombe was going to do the news. We-ell—I couldn't let him do the French crisis with no mouth, now could I? (*He mimes—as if toothless*) Anyway! It's lovely to see you all! (*He goes to kiss Reston*) Merry Christmases all round and let's hope Santa looks like Clint Eastwood. (*His momentum takes him towards Moore, who recoils in alarm*) Hallo.

Connie Oh, this is Christopher Moore, friend of Barbara's. Ray Lacey—the best make-up man in London.

Lacey Face fixer to the famous. I give them eternal beauty—so long as they don't smile.

Moore What long eyelashes you have, Mr Lacey.

Lacey You noticed. All the better to Varda you with, my dear. D'you like them? Max Factor.

Moore Yes, they're most impressive.

Lacey It's just a bit of camp for Christmas. D'you like them, Paul?

Reston (*exaggeratedly*) Divine! If the eyes are the windows of the soul—

Lewis Then they must be the Venetian blinds.

Connie I like the flared trousers Ray.

Lewis The trousers are straight—it's the legs that are flared.

Lacey I thought the chestnuts were coming with the turkey.

Connie I'll just tell Barbara you're here.

Lacey Don't I get little drinkies too?

Connie I'm so sorry, Ray. (*Going to the bar*) Campari and soda, isn't it?

Lacey Natch!

Reston (*still prodding*) Mr Moore's an anthropologist—that's why he's such a keen observer.
Lacey What—strange love rites and all that, like you get in "Reveille"? Oo, I could tell you a thing or two about that, dear, without going to the pygmies.
Moore Yes, I have rather tended to overlook the pygmies myself.
Lacey Now tell me, is there a Mrs Anthropology?
Moore No.
Lacey But anthropology must teach you a lot about human relationships, how marriage works and people live together and affairs break up. That's so, isn't it Paul?
Reston Oh yes, they're all-knowing these anthropologists. Very good with the ladies especially.
Lacey Then why isn't there a Misses?
Moore Does an asprin go looking for a headache?
Connie }
Barnes } Shame!
Lacey Acid with it!
Moore I suppose you learn a great deal about human nature yourself working in the motion picture studios.
Lacey Well no. I don't work in films actually. Not that I couldn't mind you. All the movie stars I do—you know—for television interviews and that—they all say I give them a better face than anyone they know. I must get a film a month offered to me.
Moore But you don't want to leave television, surely.
Lacey Don't I dear! You just try me.

Connie brings Lacey's drink

Thank you, darling. (*Indicates the drink*) It's the colour I like—goes with anything.

Connie exits to the kitchen

Moore You were saying.
Barnes Now, you don't want to be bored by all our shop talk—
Moore Oh but I'm never bored by shop talk—other people's, that is.
Lacey No, well, you see—I have these contracts in television. Well, everyone else would be very sweet and let me out of their silly old contract . . .
Barnes Now Ray, I know what you're going to say . . .
Lewis Same old record.
Lacey Nobody asked you. (*Continuing, to Moore*) In fact there's one producer, who shall be nameless, who promised he was going to have another word with his leading lady.
Barnes Ray!
Lacey . . . Aujourd'hui.
Barnes Ray, you know it's not my fault. If it were up to me . . .

Barbara enters

Barbara Ray, darling!
Lacey Barbara darling!

Barbara and Lacey embrace

Lacey Now Jack—a word in your ear—
Barnes (*craftily*) I'll just see if Connie needs any help in the kitchen. (*He goes to the door*)
Lacey When you get there she'll need help.

Behind Barbara's back as he is embracing her, Lacey tries vainly to pluck at Barnes as he passes. Barnes avoids him and Lacey turns his attention back to Barbara

Barnes exits to the kitchen

Don't you look fantastic, darling—and all your own work, too.
Barbara Look who taught me.
Lacey Oh isn't she sweet! And you've got that gorgeous little number on again.
Barbara What d'you mean—again?
Lacey Oh you can fool some of the people some of the time but you can't fool little Ray. You wore it once before, at Andrew's party, remember?
Barbara (*disconcerted, but smiling*) What sharp eyes you have, grandmama. All right everybody—now we're all here. Connie! Jack. Food's in the study and dining room. Champagne's on its way.
All Champagne!

Connie and Barnes enter, carrying bottles of champagne. Cheers from everyone

Barbara Is it cold enough, Jack?
Barnes As cool as another man's secretary.

Triggered by Barbara, Connie and Barnes go into the study

Lacey (*offering Reston his arm*) Hey, gorgeous! You can take me into dinner.
Reston Oh my gawd!

Lacey and Reston exit to the study

Barbara and Moore are left alone

Moore So all your guests have arrived?
Barbara Yes, there's nobody else to come.
Moore Then our prankster is here.
Barbara But they're all friends! You can't believe it's one of them.
Moore On the contrary, I can believe it could be any one of them. Shall we go in? (*He offers her his arm*)

Moore and Barbara start towards the study. The doorbell rings. Barbara freezes, terrified

Moore raises his eyebrows, and exits to the hall

CURTAIN

SCENE 3

The same. One minute later.
Barbara stands where she did at the end of Scene Two. Moore stands by the door with a long-haired young man in the latest gear. The young man holds a camera case by a long strap. Connie is by the study doorway.

Dave (*with a slight cockney accent*) Look, what is all this? I'm Dave Ogden of publicity.
Moore Don't either of you know him?
Barbara I've never seen him before.
Dave I got a call an hour ago telling me to come and cover your Christmas Party, eight o'clock tonight.
Barbara I didn't call you. And you didn't, Connie?
Connie No.
Dave Then who did?

Barnes appears in the study doorway

Connie Jack, did you?
Barnes No. (*Speaking off into the study*) Did any of you?
Reston (*off*) Did any of us what?
Barnes Did anyone order a photographer for tonight?
Reston (*off*) No.
Lewis (*off*) No.

Lacey enters

Lacey No.
Moore This gentleman says he's from your publicity department. Have you ever seen him before?
Barnes No—and I thought I knew everyone in Publicity.
Lacey So did I . . . (*He eyes Dave speculatively*)
Dave Ah well, you see, I've only been with them a week.
Lacey You mean I've already wasted six days?
Dave I joined from Hornsey Art School.

Barbara reacts to this

Moore Don't you know who called you?

Dave I dunno. Mate of mine took the call while I was out and left a message. (*He looks around the room appreciatively*) Here, this is great, innit! Very Christmassy, like!

Barnes exits to the study

Moore How did you get the address?
Dave It was on the message, wonnit?
Barbara Didn't you have to talk to your boss before coming?—
Dave Andrews? No, he'd cleared off early, hadn't he?
Moore Who left the message for you?
Dave Billy Johnson. Couldn't hardly read his writing—must have done it with his foot, I think.

Moore queries Barbara with a look

Barbara I've never had any trouble with Johnson's writing.
Moore So you got the message, came haring down from the fourth floor . . .
Dave Sixth. We're on the sixth.
Moore Yes, of course, the sixth floor. You came haring down from the sixth floor, bumped into the poor old commissionaire . . .
Dave No, we don't have them. I did bump into that dishy blonde receptionist though—very nice that was—I mean she really can bump. Then I jumped into a taxi and here I am—at the wrong house.

Reston enters

Reston What is going on?
Connie It's obviously a mistake. Somebody got their lines crossed about tomorrow.
Reston I think the least we can do is ask him to stay for a drink.
Barbara (*hopefully*) Perhaps he doesn't drink.
Dave Yeah, I do—I quite like it.
Lacey I've got a better idea—why don't we ask him to the party! After all, he has had to turn out on Christmas Eve.
Dave Oh great! I'd love that, I really would!
Barbara Oh I'm sure you've got more exciting things to do.
Dave No, I haven't.
Lacey What could he possibly have to do that's more exciting than us.
Dave (*imitates Lacey's camp style*) Right.
Barbara But oughtn't you to be getting back to the office?
Dave No—this is my last job of the night.
Moore (*taking over*) Then I'm sure Miss Love would be delighted to have you. Isn't that so, Barbara?
Barbara (*looking at Moore*) Yes—yes, of course. You must stay.
Reston It's all right now, daddy says so.
Dave Oh thanks!
Lacey Come on then, let's have your coat off—for a start.

Lacey helps Dave off with his coat, then goes to the hall to leave it, and returns
Connie exits to the study

Dave Oh this is great. Just for a bit though—I've got to get back to Greenford.
Barbara (*noting the reference*) Greenford?

Lacey takes a glass from the bar, goes to the study and returns with it full of champagne for Dave

Dave Yeah—that's where we live! We've got a house on the new estate.

Barnes and Connie enter

Lacey We? (*Disappointed*) Don't tell me you're married.
Dave Give us a chance! I'm only seventeen, you know.

Lewis enters

Moore There's a refreshing point of view.
Dave I want a few trial runs first. Time's getting on, mind you. I'll be eighteen next month.
Lacey Oh? What date?
Dave Seventh.
Lacey Capricorn! Strong, practical, aggressive.

Lacey reclines in an armchair facing Dave. Barbara turns away sharply to get a cigarette

Dave (*raising his glass*) Cheers! Merry Christmas!
All Merry Christmas!

Dave sips his champagne appreciatively

Dave That doesn't really work, does it, that astrology lark?
Lacey Oh indeed it does! It's a very exact science.
Lewis If Lacey's horoscope says 'Be prepared' he takes the pill.
Reston Do anthropologists believe in the stars, Mr Moore?
Moore Signs and portents have been part of human belief for as far back as we can trace. One cannot dismiss the fact.
Reston That's not what I asked? Do you believe in astrology yourself?
Moore No, but I realize it can influence the behaviour of those who do.
Lewis That's just what I mean about Lacey.
Barnes That's perfectly true. It's what you believe that counts. I once did a programme where three men got drunk on tonic water because they'd been told it had gin in it.
Lacey That's nothing. I remember once Lewis staying sober because he thought his gin had tonic water in it.
Lewis That's rich coming from you, darling. One Cherry B and you're anybody's.

Lacey I'm certainly not yours, duckie!
Lewis Thank God for that!
Connie Come on you two. You'll have Mr Ogden wondering what sort of firm he's joined.
Dave No, honest—I think a bit of kidding is great. But there was something I wanted to ask—about the stars and that.

Barbara is watching him carefully

Barbara What sort of thing?
Dave Well—you know how certain whatdoyoucallems—signs—are supposed to be good for each other. You know, like if you're one sign you go well together with a person of another sign?
Lacey That's called astral compatibility.
Dave Yeah, very likely. Well, I was wondering if it worked the other way, too.
Barbara How d'you mean?
Dave Well, if there are signs that don't go together—you know, so that people automatically hate each other. I mean if there's anything in it at all, you might be born to hate one certain person in the world. Well, they might be in China or somewhere like that, so you wouldn't have to worry. I mean you may never meet them as long as you live. But suppose they lived in your town—and you bumped into them one day . . .

There is a silence. Barbara seems very uneasy

Barbara What a sick thought!
Reston Maybe that's what happened to me and my wife!
Barbara Look, I'm going to give you all one more glass of champagne and then you must eat.

Barbara exits to the study

Lacey (*rallying*) But it's quite wrong. The stars are for friendship not hate. And they really do work. Tell you what! Let's have a peep what Lord Luck had to say about us all today and see if he was right. (*He crosses to desk, picks up copy of* "*Daily Express*") Here we are. Now I spent the entire morning making up that terrible old bitch Meg Lewis. Let's see what it says about me: "A perfect day for mending ancient mistakes". There, you see!

Connie snatches the paper from him

Connie You're making it up. Let me see that! Well—you'd read it earlier.

Barbara enters with champagne

Barnes What does mine say?
Connie Let me see, you're Gemini aren't you? "Resist the temptation to settle old scores today".
Barnes Oh that's easy. There are too many of them to get round to!

Reston That doesn't usually deter you.
Barnes Now that's not true. Connie, am I vindictive?

Connie does not answer him

Connie Mr Moore, what are you?
Moore Leo.
Lacey (*admiringly*) Wouldn't you know!
Reston You don't believe in the stars but you know your sign.
Moore I don't believe in income tax but I know my code number.
Connie (*reading*) "You may be in for a surprise before you go to bed".
Moore I am not in a state of surprise.
Lacey No—and you're not in bed yet, Mr Moore. Give it time, give it time.

Reston takes the paper from Connie

Reston (*to Lewis*) You're Pisces aren't you, Don?
Lacey Ah yes, the fishy one!
Reston "Minor irritants may get you down today."
Lewis (*looking at Lacey*) You can say that again!
Lacey Minor irritants may get you down today.
Connie Come on Paul, what does yours say?
Reston "Your pride may get you into trouble this evening."
Lacey Yes, you have got very haughty lately.
Barnes (*with friendly sarcasm*) Pride? He doesn't know the meaning of the word.
Reston Quite right. I don't.
Barnes I still say your last show wasn't up to scratch.
Reston (*bristling instantly*) My last show was damned g—
Lacey He always bites, doesn't he!

They laugh. He gets the point and grins ruefully

Reston Anyway that's not pride. It's professional satisfaction.
Dave No, I know what he means. If anyone criticizes my pictures, I get very up tight.
Lacey Up what, dear?
All Tight.
Lacey Oooh . . .
Barnes Here, let's have a look at Barbara's.
Barbara Oh Lord, must you?
Barnes (*to Barbara*) Yours say "Tonight you could enter a whole new world".
Barbara I know—we've finally sold the show to America.
Barnes Now Barbara, you know I never mix business with pleasure.
Reston Unless you're firing someone.
Barnes That's slander! Connie, am I not the dolliest producer you've worked with?
Lacey Oh come now—you don't want her telling fibs on Christmas Eve, do you? Anyway, we haven't read Davie's horoscope yet. (*He takes the*

paper) Capricorn—Cap—"Beware of giving way to impulse today, it could get you into trouble". What have you been up to?

Barbara bustles, a little too brightly

Barbara Come on now, that's enough of that nonsense. No-one's started on the food yet.
All Food.
Connie And I've been slaving away over a hot delicatessen all morning.
Barbara (*attracting Moore's attention*) Christopher!
Lewis (*to Dave*) Bring your camera—it'll improve our table manners (*He hands Dave his camera*)
Lacey (*to Dave*) Oh Dave, this is my best side.

Lewis snatches the camera back

Lewis I've had second thoughts.
Lacey Pity your father didn't.

Dave, Lacey, Lewis, Reston, Barnes and Connie exit to the study

Barbara Are you certain it's someone at the party?
Moore Yes I am.
Barbara Then that settles it. I'm going to call it off.
Moore No you're not!
Barbara Well I'm not going to stand around like a sacrificial lamb.
Moore Whoever it is would only choose another time and another place and I can't be with you twenty-four hours a day.
Barbara (*with a shiver*) Then how do you suggest I get through the evening?
Moore Well you're the performer.
Barbara And you're the detective. Have you any ideas at all?
Moore Yes, one or two.
Barbara Who?
Moore Oh they're not as definite as who. Just one or two vague theories as to why. You seem to keep them on a pretty tight rein.
Barbara (*astonished*) A tight rein!
Moore Yes.
Barbara Christopher—have you any idea of what running a show like mine means? I am the show. It's all on me. We work as a team but I have to be the captain.
Moore Teams have a way of breaking up. Yours seems to stick together.
Barbara They're very loyal.
Moore There are different ways of enforcing loyalty.
Barbara Can it be enforced?
Moore I should say so—yes.
Barbara How?
Moore One way is by knowing where the body's buried.
Barbara Superintendent—I do not keep my team together by blackmail. And I think your choice of phrase is a little gruesome.

Moore I'm sorry. I didn't mean that you retained your colleagues by blackmail. I really didn't.

Barnes enters from the study followed by Lewis. Lewis is trying to crack a nut with his teeth

Barnes Nutcrackers—are there some in the kitchen?
Barbara In the blue unit. There's more food in there too.

Lacey enters from the study with two glasses of champagne, and moves to Moore and Barbara

Lewis It's all right Jack. Lacey, crack that with your eyelashes, will you?
Lacey I've got a better idea. Why don't you read it one of your serious stories and it'll split itself laughing. Champagne?

Connie enters with name cards and goes upstairs. Barnes goes to the hall. Lewis follows to the door, whispering "Once upon a time" to the nut he is holding

Lacey (*giving champagne to Moore and Barbara*) What are you two doing, forming a splinter group?

Connie puts name cards in each of the bedrooms

Moore No, it's just that we've got a lot to catch up on.
Lacey (*slyly*) I see . . .

Barnes enters from the hall with nutcrackers and a plate of canapés and crosses to the study

Barnes (*giving the plate to Lewis*) Got them.

Lewis puts a long tubular canapé in his mouth

Lewis Smoked salmon.

Barnes exits to the study

Lacey whips out a Dunhill, and holds it to Lewis's canapé

Lacey Want a light?
Lewis Confucius say: faggot should not play with fire.
Reston (*to Lacey*) Oh, you've got the champagne!

Lewis goes upstairs and talks to Connie

Reston and Dave enter. They go with Lacey to the foot of the stairs and talk quietly

Barbara Does that look as if they're terrified?
Moore I didn't say they were terrified.
Barbara What are you suggesting then?
Moore Sometimes just the fact you know something about a person is enough to make them scared. Even if you never mention it. The threat's in their mind rather than yours.
Barbara I think I know what you mean, but it's not like that . . .
Moore Lewis, for instance. You see, I get the impression that he feels threatened—and not just by his contract.
Barbara (*after a pause*) Oh it's absurd! Don knows I'm not threatening him.
Moore Ah, but not threatening him with what? (*Pause*) Look, I give you my word anything you tell me will go no further. (*Pause*) Believe me, I need to know if I'm to protect you.
Barbara You promise you won't go all professional about it?
Moore Of course.
Barbara (*after a long pause*) He did knock a woman down that time. She was badly injured. They never found Don.
Moore I see. And what about Barnes—the corruption at the BBC. You said he was acquitted. That was another white lie, wasn't it?
Barbara No, he was acquitted. But he was guilty. He did take the bribes.
Moore Does anyone else know about these things?
Barbara No, I'm the only one.
Moore How did you find out?
Barbara They needed to tell someone. You see, I really am a very good Auntie type—people confide in me.

Connie and Lacey come downstairs. The group breaks up. Reston and Dave look for a record in the record-player cabinet

Reston You're imagining things.
Dave I'm not—it's a code. Miss Love, have you got that Pop Opera by the Who?

Barbara's attitude becomes strained again

Barbara Yes . . . it's over there on the left-hand side.
Reston Pop opera by the Who . . .
Dave (*to Barbara*) Thank you.
Lacey (*to Reston*) Here Paul, have one of these, they're delish.
Reston No thanks, Ray.
Lacey You haven't eaten a thing all evening.
Reston I'm not hungry.
Dave Now then—You take the first letter of the last word, the second letter of the next to last word. See, it says "Politicians" . . .

Dave and Reston exit to the study

Reston (*off*) Let me see that . . . He's right, you know, look—"Politicians are . . ." What's this?

Lacey exits to the study
Lewis chases Connie off to the kitchen

(*off*) Ray, Jack, listen to this . . .
Lacey (*off*) Politicians are *what*?

There is a burst of laughter off in the study

Moore He seems an appealing young man, don't you think?
Barbara What?
Moore Young Ogden.
Barbara Oh—yes—I suppose he is. I haven't given it much thought.
Moore Then why does he upset you?
Barbara Well, it's obvious, isn't it? I said it would be a stranger, and he's a stranger.
Moore No, I mean apart from that. There's something else, isn't there?
Barbara No . . . nothing.

Barnes enters from the study and exits to the kitchen

Moore My dear Barbara, years of training have given me the instincts of a ferret. That young man disturbs you in some special way. It's in your own interests to tell me what it is. I'm about to make some enquiries about him. You might give me a line to pursue.
Barbara Oh, it's absurd, I know. I have a feeling about him, that's all. I can't explain it. I know you don't deal in feelings.
Moore Oh, but I do. Feelings are sometimes merely facts which just haven't happened yet. Have you got another telephone?
Barbara Yes, there's one upstairs. My private number. What are you going to do?
Moore I'm going to find out if that young man is what he says he is. (*He goes upstairs*)
Barbara It's in my bedroom. Along the landing and the door facing you.
Moore Thank you. I'll find it.
Barbara Don't be long.
Moore (*from the landing*) I won't be. Don't worry. Nothing will happen yet. Watching you squirm is part of it for this kind of chap.

Moore exits along the landing
After a pause, Barbara moves to the hall and bumps into Barnes, who is entering quietly from the kitchen.

Barbara Oh Jack, you did make me jump.
Barnes Sorry, Barbara my darling. Super party, as always.
Barbara Thank you, Jack. I always feel a bit guilty about taking you away from Jennie on Christmas Eve.
Barnes Not at all! Jennie's fine. She has her sisters down for the holiday and they'll be sitting with her. They'll natter on for hours without missing me. Besides, I won't be too late if you don't mind.

Barbara Of course I don't.
Barnes You shouldn't be too late yourself. You look a bit off-colour to me. Are you sure you're feeling all right?
Barbara Yes, thank you Jack. Just tired, I expect.
Barnes Not ready to sell out to me yet?
Barbara (*with a smile*) Now Jack, don't start that again.
Barnes Just thought maybe I'd caught you at a low ebb.
Barbara Jack, the day I'm that low, I'll be walking under croquet hoops on tiptoe.
Barnes Yes, or six feet under.
Barbara What!
Barnes Well—I mean—I know what my chances are.
Barbara Yes, I see . . .
Barnes Nothing worrying you, is there?
Barbara What makes you think that?
Barnes I just thought maybe someone might have been—bothering you.
Barbara (*a little shrilly*) What d'you mean, bothering me?
Barnes Well—I thought, maybe—Reston.
Barbara No, no—nothing like that.

Lewis enters from kitchen

Lewis Ho Ho Ho! Plots! Conspiracies!
Barnes Nothing of the kind, you neurotic doodler. I was just telling Barbara she should take things easy. She looks a little tired.
Lewis That's what the Ansaphone does for you.
Barbara (*alarmed*) The Ansa . . .
Lewis You must admit I warned you.
Barbara I don't understand.
Lewis Get one of those devilish contraptions, I said, and you'll never know another moment's peace. You get home from a gruelling day of telephone purgatory and what do you find? Another half hour of crisply capsuled hell waiting for you in your drawing room.
Barbara Yes, of course—you did warn me. (*She makes a determined effort at gaiety*) Now will everyone please stop worrying about my health and please get on with the party! It's more like a surgery than a celebration!

Moore enters on the landing

Moore Have you got an STD directory?
Barbara Yes, there's one in the bedside drawer.
Moore Thank you.
Lewis You'll find the Pygmies at Littlehampton two-three-two.
Moore I'll tell them you'll be late home.

Moore exits along the landing, as Reston, Lacey and Dave erupt out of the study in animated discussion
Connie enters from the kitchen

Lacey I tell you it does work, I've seen it work!
Reston It's pure self-deception.
Dave I've never even heard of it.
Speaking together

Lacey Barbara—tell them about the Ouija board. You remember—that time we played with the glass and the letters.

Barbara Oh that! We were just fooling around.

Lacey Yes, but the most sensational things happened. Don't you remember?

Connie Yes, I do. It was extraordinary. It told me things about me I didn't even know myself.

Reston That's just your subconscious coming through.

Lewis Oh my God, if we're going to get Lacey's subconscious the police will come and raid us.

Lacey Why don't you take a swim in a pair of lead knickers? Where are the cards, Barbara? You know, the ones with the letters of the alphabet on them.

Barbara I don't know. Connie put them away somewhere.

Connie (*taking some cards from the bar drawer*) Yes, here they are.

Lacey Good. Now then, who's on for a spot of the occult?

Dave Yeah.

Lacey Yes. Let's use the coffee table.

Barbara It's not exactly a party game, is it?

Lacey Of course it's a party game. It's the best possible party game. We all get to touch fingers. (*He touches Reston*)

Barbara I don't know. I think it's dangerous.

Barnes Oh don't be such an old party poop.

Lacey Just sit down and have yourself a ball.

Barnes Connie, you can get to sit on my knee.

They spread out the cards on the coffee-table and arrange seats round it

Connie No thanks, not without a safety belt.

Lacey Ooops, glass. Must have a glass. (*He fetches a brandy glass from the bar then goes to the light switch*) Paul—keep me a seat next to you. (*He switches off all the lights except those on the tree*)

Barbara No. I'm sorry, I want the lights on.

Lacey But we won't have any mysterioso.

Barbara Put this one on here, Jack. That'll give Ray all the mysterioso he needs.

Lewis Otherwise he might disappear up his own aura.

Lacey switches on a bracket lamp from the main switch. Barnes adjusts the lamp

Lacey Well that's better than talking out of it as you do!

Lacey puts the glass upside down on the table and sits with the others. The telephone bell rings. Barbara answers it

Barbara (*into the phone*) Hello?

Lewis First time I've known them try to get through by telephone.

Barbara (*putting the phone down*) Wrong number. (*She sits again*)

Connie Probably our regular burglar checking in.
Reston Talking about burglars, where's our eminent anthropologist, by the way?
Barbara Put your claws in darling, you'll scratch the furniture.
Lacey Quiet! Quiet, please! This is very serious.
Lewis I thought you said it was just a bit of fun.
Lacey It's a very serious bit of fun. Now then. Little pools of hush. All right, now everyone rest a finger on top of the glass. Just rest it very gently, don't press. Now then, very quiet please. And concentrate. (*He pauses and closes his eyes dramatically*) If there's anyone there who has a message for us, please move the glass.

Nothing happens. Connie giggles. They all break up. Lacey glares. He pauses then starts again

If there is anyone in the spirit world who has a message, please move the glass.

Again nothing happens. Then suddenly the glass starts to move in circles, slowly at first and then faster

Dave Hey, it's moving!
Lacey Shhh!

The glass suddenly darts towards a letter, back to the middle, darts to another letter and so on. They call the letters out as the glass touches them

All B . . . U . . . M. Bum.
Lacey (*shrill with indignation*) Bum? Bum! What sort of message is that?
Lewis Bum. Seems perfectly clear to me.
Dave It's a rude little spirit, innit?
Lacey Somebody's not playing fair! Somebody's pushing or shoving! And I've got a pretty shrewd idea who it is. (*He glares at Lewis*) Unless we all play fair there's no use going on.
Barbara (*trying to hide her laughter*) Now then, come on everybody. Stop it whoever it is and let's start again.
Lacey Concentrate this time.

They put their fingers on the glass again. Nobody except Lacey is taking it seriously. After a pause it starts to move again in circles then darts towards the letters

All B . . . A . . . R . . . B . . . A

The glass stops

Lacey It's trying to get through to Barbara. Concentrate.

The glass starts again

All B . . . A . . .

The glass goes in circles and stops again

Dave It can't get through.

Suddenly the glass starts to move again, this time at great speed

All L . . . O . . . V . . . E. Love. L . . . I . . . E . . . S. Lies. B . . . L . . . E . . . E . . . D . . . I . . . N . . . G. Bleeding.

Reston Love lies bleeding. What does that mean?

The lights go out abruptly to complete blackout

All (*jumping up*) What's up? . . . Hey—what's happened to the lights? Who did that? . . .

Suddenly the sinister Ansaphone voice cuts through. The other voices cease

Voice Miss Love? . . . Miss Barbara Love?

Barbara and Connie emit a long bloodcurdling scream

The CURTAIN *is crept down during the scream. At the end of the scream the house lights are instantly switched full on and the audience finds itself facing the curtain.*

ACT II

Scene 1

The same. Immediately following.

The CURTAIN *goes up in darkness. The lights come on immediately, revealing everyone scattered about the room. Moore is on the balcony, looking down.*

Moore Barbara! Are you all right?

Barbara Yes, thank you. I feel such an idiot. I haven't screamed like that since I was a child.

Connie Who put the lights out?

Barnes And what was that voice?

Reston Yes, who was that? Was it supposed to be a joke?

Barnes Damn silly joke if you ask me.

Lewis It was Lacey playing silly beggars—trying to get us at it with that tape recorder.

Moore (*downstairs by now, watchful*) Was it you, Lacey?

Lacey No, of course it wasn't. I'll tell you what it was, though. I think we'd made an actual contact. There was a presence in this room. We shouldn't stop now, we should press on.

Barnes Oh, come on, Ray—you can see how Barbara feels.

All Barbara wants to do is to get rid of them so that she can talk to Moore

Barbara No please—I don't want to spoil the fun. Look, why don't you use the big table in the kitchen?

Reston No, I'm not going to leave you alone at your own party.

Lewis Lacey can go and hold hands with himself.

Barbara No really, I'll feel stupid if you all sit around being kind. Anyway, I have the presents to sort out.

Reston We'll stay and help.

Connie (*looks to Moore for guidance and gets the nod*) No, I know how Barbara feels. I'd be the same. Let's get out of her hair for a bit.

Lacey Well, if you're sure it's all right. Connie, you bring the cards. The atmosphere is perfect. I think we could make a real breakthrough to-night. Come on, David, this includes you.

They collect up the cards and glass, and open up the seats

Dave No, I'd rather not.

Lacey Don't be such a cissy.

Barnes (*to Barbara*) You take it easy, d'you hear?

Barbara Yes, I will.

Reston You staying here, are you, Moore?

Moore Yes, I think my vibrations would strike the wrong note.

Reston There's nothing wrong with your vibrations, Moore, I'd say you were B-sharp.

They all go to the kitchen except Barbara and Moore

Moore Could you tell who did that voice?
Barbara No. There was a nasty little message too.
Moore Yes: "Love lies bleeding". I heard it. I'm sorry you were so frightened. But at least I warned you I was going to switch off the lights.
Barbara You rang off too quickly. I was going to say don't do it.
Moore You might have given something away.
Barbara Do you think someone suspects you're a policeman?
Moore We must regard that as a possibility. For instance, before the game—did anyone ask where I was?
Barbara Yes. Paul Reston did.
Moore Reston. Where was he sitting?
Barbara There. Next to me. What were you after when you switched off the lights?
Moore I wanted to precipitate something and I did. You were in no danger.
Barbara No danger! He could have stabbed me, shot me—anything!
Moore Not this fellow. Not with a room full of people. Fingerprints, the risk of blood on his hands. No, he intends to strangle you. You heard him say so.
Barbara And you believe him?
Moore I believe everything that man says. He's just that kind of psychotic. He wants to tell us exactly what he's going to do, then do it despite us.

Barbara breaks down

I'm sorry, this won't do. This is just what he wants.
Barbara I know. It's just that . . . Oh Christopher, whoever it is, they're beginning to get me. You've got to find them, you've got to stop them.
Moore Don't worry, I will.
Barbara I'm really frightened now. I can feel it getting nearer—moving in on me.
Moore Come on now—where's the cool, calm auntie who enchanted me on the television? She'd eat this chap for elevenses. He wants to get you rattled. You mustn't let him.
Barbara I'm sorry. I'll try. Did you find out anything about Ogden?
Moore They're still digging. I'm waiting for them to call me back.
Barbara I don't think it is Ogden. I'm sure now it's one of the others.

Connie opens the hatch from the kitchen

Connie Ray's dragging us down to the wine cellar. He says it's spookier down there. Will you be all right?

The telephone rings upstairs

Barbara Yes, Connie.

Connie closes the hatch

Moore Oh, that'll be for me. I gave them your private number. I won't be long. (*He goes upstairs to the landing*)
Barbara Christopher . . .
Moore (*reassuringly*) Two minutes.

Barbara sits anxiously, nervous and preoccupied

Dave enters behind her. He has his camera strap in his hands

Barbara jumps
Dave closes the door carefully. Barbara is like a mouse watching a cat.

Dave All alone, are you?
Barbara Mr Moore will be down in a minute. He's just upstairs making a telephone call.
Dave Oh yes?
Barbara Where are the others?
Dave They're still in the cellar. I just came to get my camera. (*He picks up the camera*) Only, I wanted to say how much this means to me, you see. (*He stretches the camera strap nervously between his hands*) I couldn't say it in front of the others, but I'm a fan of yours, you know. The biggest.
Barbara That's nice.
Dave Yeah—I think you're the best thing on the box. I never miss a show.
Barbara Surely you're a little old for my show?
Dave Well—yeah—I s'pose I am, really. It's just that I started watching it when I was twelve and I've been hooked on it ever since.
Barbara That's wonderful. I must tell Mr Barnes. He'll be delighted. He's always saying the potential age group for the show is much higher.
Dave The first time I saw you I felt a sort of thing for you. I started collecting pictures of you. I've got about seven hundred now. I sit in my room and study them.
Barbara Doesn't your girl friend get jealous?
Dave Don't joke. I read all the gossip about you, anything I can find. All the chat.
Barbara Oh you don't want to believe all that rubbish.
Dave I know what you like for your breakfast, where you go for your holidays. I know every dress you've ever worn.
Barbara Why?
Dave Well—because you're—in them—you know. But to be with you for Christmas—wow.
Barbara But you have your own party at home, you must get back to it.
Dave Oh yeah. I mean my parents always gave me a rave Christmas—ever since I can remember. 'Cos I was adopted may be . . . you know to make it up to me or something . . . can sometimes cause emotional problems. But this well, this is like when people talk about a dream coming true. Only they don't usually do they?
Barbara Sometimes they do.
Dave No. Not really. I mean you can dream about something in your mind

for a long time and when you finally do it, well, it's not the same—not the same at all. Why is that?

Barbara Well I suppose because in our minds we can . . . make things exactly as we want them to be . . . but in life we can't.

Dave Yeah, but this you see, well this is just as good as the dream.

Barbara I'm glad. (*She rises*) Here, let me get you some more champagne.

Dave No thanks.

Barbara Something to eat perhaps.

She moves, he blocks her

Dave No thanks.

Barbara Well I think I'd like some more champagne.

She moves towards study, but again he blocks her

I said I think I'd like some champagne.

Again she makes for the study. Again he blocks her

Dave I was wondering—I mean, I know I have all these pictures of you, like I said. But what would really be great would be if I could just—take one of you myself—you know, my own picture, like—to preserve, like, you know.

Barbara That's a very sweet idea. I'll just go and fix my hair.

Dave No—you're just fine as you are. Here, I think, down here.

He shepherds her across. She sits. He stands over her and sets her shoulders the way he wants them. She shrinks. We see that the little finger of his left hand is stiff and set at an angle. He is measuring her with an exposure meter

What's up? Oh, my finger, is it? S'nothing to worry about. I was born with it. "Another potential emotional problem" says Dr Farnesbarnes. Never worried me though. They're half barmy these trick cyclists, you know. Now, then, you just sit there and I'll get the old Brownie out.

He moves behind her, camera strap stretched between his hands. She whips round

Barbara No! (*She rises*)

Moore enters on the landing

Moore Ogden! Having a little photographic session, are we?

Dave Yeah! I thought I'd take my own pin-ups for Christmas.

Moore Don't let me interrupt. (*He comes downstairs*)

Barbara No, it's not a very good idea—

Moore Oh but it is! Do carry on.

Dave I'm sorry, I didn't mean to be a nuisance. I just got carried away.

Moore Now then, where were we.

Dave No, it's all right. I don't think Miss Love's in the mood.

Moore Nonsense! Provided a woman is drawing breath and in full make-up she's in the mood. Perhaps reclining here. That would be rather fetching . . . (*He arranges Barbara*) Don't you think so, Ogden?

Dave Yeah—that's fine.

Moore And for the full touch of Edwardian fragrance, I think a little something in the hands, don't you? Some trifle to toy with—wouldn't you say? A silk handkerchief? (*With a flourish he produces his own from his fob*)

Dave No, it's not my style.

Moore No—a bit too like an influenza commercial.

Barbara is now watching closely

Now let's see—a book, perhaps? Idly leafing through the pages of a book? (*He tries a book from the desk*)

Dave Look, forget it.

Moore No, too literary. Something more personal is what we require—ah! I have the very thing. (*He rummages in the desk drawer*)
How about—this, Ogden? (*He throws the grotesque doll to Dave*)

Dave catches the doll, looks at it, flicks a frightened glance first at Moore then at Barbara, drops the doll, and bolts through the living-room doors. A second later, the front door slams

Barbara is shivering

Barbara Aren't you going after him?

Moore It's not necessary. They'll pick him up.

Barbara When you were upstairs—he was so creepy. (*She shivers*)

Moore He probably wouldn't have harmed you.

Barbara Probably?

Moore He's known.

Barbara What did you mean—he's known?

Moore He's known to his local police station. They say he's quite harmless.

Barbara Do they.

Moore The facts are that he does work in your Publicity Department and he did join them from the Art College a week ago. He was in trouble while he was still at the College for pestering celebrities to take their photographs. It's a fetish with him. And he was once at the centre of a scandal at the College when he sent an obscene doll to one of the female teachers.

Barbara What will happen to him?

Moore He might get a suspended sentence. It depends on the medical report. They might take the view that he's now the right man in the right job—likely to settle down. What puzzles me though, is his particular fixation on you. I wondered if you could account for it?

Barbara (*avoiding his eyes*) No, I'm afraid not. One's always vulnerable to that kind of thing . . . When I think of how the evening began—I don't know how to thank you.

Moore Don't think about it any more. I shall need a statement from you tomorrow, of course. Tonight I should just go on with your party. I'll

let you know when I want you to come down to the station.
Barbara Oh please, won't you stay?
Moore I really must be getting back.
Barbara Just one more whisky. (*She goes to the bar*)

Unseen by them, the main room doors are slowly and furtively slid shut

Moore Your logic is overpowering. I have no doubt my lot down at the station will be drinking it out of their helmets by now.
Barbara Now you must have something to eat. You haven't had a chance all evening and there's tons of food in the study.
Moore Well you haven't eaten anything either.

Moore exits into study

Barbara No. I'd better see what the others are doing. Oh I feel like a *real* party now! (*She opens the doors to the hall*)

The whole party jumps out at her wearing grotesque masks and party hats and shouting "Boo!" She jumps. They all start chanting "We want Santa Claus!" Barbara backs away as they start advancing on her. They are rather high. They continue to chant "We want Santa Claus" each time she turns her back and freeze every time she turns to face them. She eventually catches them out and they cheer. Moore runs out of the study

Lacey Prezzy time! We want our prezzies!
Barnes (*to Moore*) Take no notice. It's just the television executive class at play.
Barbara (*to Moore*) It's a silly little game we do. It started on the show with the kids and now it's become a kind of tradition.
Connie We hide little cards with their names all over the house.
Lewis When you find your card you rush back here.
Reston And Santa Claus gives you your present.
Moore Santa Claus being?
Barbara Me.
All Auntie!
Barbara Whiskers and all.
Lewis (*to Moore*) Cute, huh?
Lacey Oh don't be such an old misery-drawers! Come on, prezzy time. Where's that sweet boy?
Barbara He had to go.
Lacey What a pity. Still never mind.
Lewis He said he'd like to call you but he couldn't think what.
Lacey Your face is hanging out again. Right. Let's go. Get your drag on, girl.
Barbara Connie have you hidden the cards?
Connie Yes, they're all in the upstairs rooms.
Lacey All right, men! You all know what you have to do!
Connie Barbara, d'you think you should?

Barbara Of course—I wouldn't miss it for worlds.
Connie But . . .
Barbara Now come on Connie, don't be such an old fusspot.

The men run upstairs. Reston goes into the first bedroom, Lacey and Barnes into the second. Lewis exits along the corridor

Oh, but we haven't got a present for Christopher.
Connie Yes we have. I thought . . . (*She whispers in Barbara's ear*)
Barbara Oh, what a good idea! Off you go, Christopher—there's a card for you, too.
Moore (*running upstairs*) I haven't had so much fun since my sergeant had his patrol car towed away.

Moore exits along the corridor

Barbara Where's my costume? (*She goes upstairs*)
Connie It's in your wardrobe.

Barbara goes along landing and off. Connie starts tape-recorder, which plays "Jingle Bells", and switches out room lights except for tree and wall bracket. She goes upstairs and along landing where she bumps into Lewis. Lacey comes out of second bedroom and into first as Lewis goes into second bedroom. Reston runs out of first room and along landing and off. Lacey and Lewis emerge simultaneously, and collide. Lewis screams:

Lewis My God! The human meringue!

Lewis exits along the landing. Lacey comes furtively downstairs. Barnes comes out of second room and into first. Lacey appears at living room doors, looks round, then goes off to the study. Barbara's voice from upstairs calls out

Barbara (*off*) Oh, Connie, don't be so silly!

Barbara enters, dressed as Santa Claus. She comes along landing and downstairs into the room to the tree. Then she starts to cross the room to the desk, but is stopped when the lights all go out, and the music stops

Who . . . No! Please!

There are sounds of a struggle, then the sound of someone being strangled. The music starts again, this time speeded up. And the struggle stops

A photo flash goes off four times, and it's possible to see something lying on the stage. There are shouts from upstairs and the landing light goes on, showing Moore at the top of the stairs. Moore, followed by Reston and

Barnes, comes into the room and stepping over the body of Santa Claus, runs into the study

The lights in the room come on, Barnes switches off the tape recorder, and Reston unties the stocking from round Santa's neck

Moore runs back on, holding a light meter

Reston She's dead!

CURTAIN

SCENE 2

The same. One hour later.

When the CURTAIN *rises, Moore is standing by the coffee table with the doll. Barnes is facing him. Lewis is sitting on a chair.*

Moore Don't be so naive, Barnes, sentiment never solved a murder.
Barnes I can't believe she's dead. I still can't believe it. I mean it's as if I could just switch on the television and there she'd be.
Moore It's simply a matter of logistics now. Where you all were when the mustic started to go wrong.
Barnes You're a cold-blooded bastard aren't you? Can't you take the damned thing away? Do you have to have it sitting there?
Moore Does it bother you?
Barnes Of course it bothers me.
Moore The doll isn't bothering you, is it?
Lewis No.
Moore Are you feeling all right?
Lewis Fine. It's just my stomach—always lets me down on these occasions.
Moore On these occasions?
Lewis Crises—emergencies.
Moore I see. Now Barnes tells me you were going downstairs just before the music started to go wrong.
Lewis That's not true.
Barnes I didn't say that.
Moore Then where were you?
Lewis I was in the utility room at the top of the house.
Moore It took you a long time to get down. You were a full minute after everybody else.
Lewis I felt ill.
Moore Ill?
Barnes His sensitive stomach, no doubt.
Moore But I thought your stomach only reacted to crises.
Lewis Yes.

Moore You didn't know at that point that this was a crisis, did you? All you knew was that something had gone wrong with the tape recorder.

Lewis Look, there was a feeling of something wrong—people tumbling down the stairs and all that mad music.

Moore Thank you. Barnes would you please call in Mr Lacey.

Lewis Is—is that all you want to know?

Moore Yes.

Barnes Ray!

Moore For the time being.

Lacey enters from the study. He has been crying

Lewis Oh, for God's sake!

Lacey Yes, I've been crying. People do, you know.

Moore Sit down, Mr Lacey, nobody's criticizing you.

Lacey He is. Mr Smallballs there—he thinks a few tears would castrate him.

Lewis You . . .

Moore I have one simple question for you, Mr Lacey. Where were you when you heard the music speed up?

Lacey (*pale smile*) In the downstairs loo in the hall.

Moore So you hadn't been upstairs?

Lacey Oh yes, I had. But I'd found my card almost at once and I'd come down to claim my present when I—you know—got a little call.

Moore So you were nearer the scene than any of us then?

Lacey Yes, I suppose I was.

Moore Yet you were the last but one to arrive.

Lacey Well . . . you can't just . . . stop—just like that, can you? Anyway, I thought it was being attended to.

Moore What made you think that?

Lacey Well, just after the music went funny, the lights went back on and I did see someone go past. I saw them through the frosted glass.

Moore From which direction?

Lacey Coming from the living room.

Moore Was this before you heard people coming downstairs?

Lacey Oh yes, just a moment before.

Moore Did you get any idea of who it could have been?

Lacey No, you can't see through that glass, you know. I did think it was about Lewis's height, though.

Lewis Oh yes, you would say that, wouldn't you . . .

Moore Thank you, Mr Lacey. Perhaps you'd call Mr Reston for me.

Lacey goes and opens the study door

Lacey Paul.

Reston enters

Moore Sit down, Reston.

Reston I'd rather stand, if you don't mind.
Moore As you wish.
Reston I do wish. I might also wish to telephone my solicitor.
Moore What on earth for? There's nothing official about this little enquiry —you'll observe I have no constable taking notes. Anyone is perfectly entitled to refuse to take part.
Reston From which you'd be perfectly entitled to draw your own conclusions.
Moore Perfectly.
Barnes We've all co-operated.
Reston I dare say. He's a cool customer our Superintendent. Turns it all into a party game. Postman's Knock. Come in one by one. Ask a little question. And meanwhile he's playing fast and loose with the Judge's Rules.
Lewis Oh come on, man.
Lacey Paul—all he wants to know is where you were when "Jingle Bells" went wrong.
Reston I was in the utility room.
Moore Ah . . .
Lewis Wait a minute, you couldn't have been. That's where I was.
Reston You certainly were not. I—no—wait a minute. No—I'd searched the utility room couldn't find my card and—yes, that's right, I'd actually gone down the landing into the place over the garage.

They all stare at him

(*To Moore*) I suppose you're drawing conclusions from that now.
Moore Not necessarily. Anyone can make a mistake.
Reston Thank you. That's very gracious of you. Now d'you mind telling me where you were at the time? When I turned the lights on, you were at the top of the stairs. You could have been going down or coming up.
Moore That's hardly relevant.
Reston Oh, isn't it? I think it's very relevant indeed. You're the odd man out here. We all know each other pretty well. Nobody knows you. You say you're a policeman but nobody's seen your warrant card.
Moore Warrant cards, Mr Reston, are for rookies. I haven't carried one for years.
Reston That's very convenient. You give us some yarn about being called in . . .
Barnes He has a point you know, Moore. I believe in good order and you haven't really established your credentials.
Moore (*with great patience*) You saw my men.
Reston (*with sudden realization which is shared by the others*) No, we didn't. You had us all cooped up in the study while someone was tramping about out here. It could have been anyone for all we know.
Moore That's easily dealt with.

Moore exits to the kitchen

There is a pause, then Barbara appears and stands framed in the doorway. She is in slight shock. Moore appears behind her

I'm sorry to have kept you waiting, Miss Love.

Barbara (*whispers*) That's all right. (*She advances into the room. She is scared. One of these four men is her would-be murderer*)

Moore (*gently*) It's all a nightmare for you, I know. Here, sit down.

He guides her into an armchair facing downstage

A little brandy. Reston.

Reston goes over to the bar to pour the brandy

There. You'll be all right in a minute.

Barbara Poor Connie . . . (*She breaks down*)

Moore Yes, I know.

Reston brings Moore the brandy. Moore hovers solicitously over Barbara with it

Here—sip this—go on, sip it.

Barbara sips

Now, when you feel able to, I'd like to clear up a little point for me.

Barbara Yes, of course. I'm all right now.

Moore Reston here is worried about my credentials.

Barbara (*weak but cold—Reston could be the murderer*) That's absurd. I called him in. (*She addresses Reston but does not look at him*) He asked Connie and me to say he was a friend. Poor Connie—it was my fault . . . (*She breaks down*)

Moore (*gently*) That's nonsense and you know it. If it was anyone's fault it was mine.

Reston Now there's an admission!

Barnes Oh shut up, man!

Barbara She said we shouldn't play the silly game. Then, when I insisted, she put on the costume herself and said she'd be Santa Claus. If I hadn't let her do that . . . (*She shudders*)

Moore (*using deliberate shock tactics*) If you hadn't let her do that then somebody in this room would have strangled you as he intended.

There is a shocked silence. Then a din of protest

Lacey That's a monstrous thing to say. } *Speaking together*
Barnes Can't you see the woman's at the end of her tether? }

Moore It happens to be the truth. I'm afraid it's only the first of many truths Miss Love is going to have to face before the evening is over.

There is again a babble of protest

Lewis You're bloody well enjoying this!

Moore rides over them

Moore Her life is at stake.

There is silence

And each one of you has a reason for wishing her—inconvenient presence removed.

Barbara (*stunned*) No.

Moore You, for instance, Barnes. Connie was your mistress. You own half the show. With Barbara out of the way and Connie to take her place . . .

Barnes That's a damned lie!

Reston No, it isn't. You were always trying to build Connie up. D'you think nobody knew of the little love-ins that went on in your big executive office? It was sickening the way you intrigued behind Barbara's back.

Barbara No, it's not true!

Barnes You're just trying to cover your own tracks. The whole studio knows you thought you had it made with Barbara.

Reston Don't be absurd!

Barnes Then your charm began to pall and she gave you your marching orders.

Barbara, looking down at the floor, in confirmation of this

And how you crawled to get taken back. It was pathetic.

Reston Crawling is something you'd know all about . . .

Lacey Oh stop it for God's sake! Connie's *dead*! It's indecent . . .

Lewis Oh, turn it up, Lacey—we all know you're the sensitive one of the party.

Moore is watching, noting, a little smug. This is what he had planned

Lacey Yes, and you're the sick one!

Lewis (*with a laugh*) *I'm* sick!

Lacey You just love seeing people tear each other to pieces.

Moore (*stirring*) Mr Lewis is a writer. Perhaps he wants to put it all in one of his novels.

Lacey Novels. He wrote one grotty little book ten years ago, that sold a hundred and fifty copies and that's his lot, duckie!

Lewis makes to explode but Moore overrides him

Lewis You . . .

Moore (*still stirring*) Oh but that's only because he hasn't had enough time. Writing the show is so demanding.

Lacey That's not a week's work for a grown man.

Lewis Now listen, you bloody fairy . . .

Moore No, I'm sure you're wrong, Mr Lacey. Mr Lewis particularly wanted to leave the show to devote more time to serious writing.

Lacey Mr Lewis wanted to leave the show because he'd been offered "Tot's Corner" by the other channel—at twice the money. And he didn't like the way Barbara read his deathless prose.

Lewis And you—what did you say about her? You said that every week making her up got more like repairing the M1. You've had it in for Barbara because you think she queered your pitch with Paul.

Reston Oh come on, Don!

Lewis No—he's been dishing it out, why shouldn't he get his too. The way he tailed after you like a lovesick girl, it was unbelievable. And because you were kind to him he thought it was the start of an immortal twosome.
Reston Don't be so bloody vicious. I wasn't being kind. I like Ray.
Lewis Liking's not what he thought you had in mind. I used to watch him. He was on Cloud Seven every time you came near him. Then Barbara snatched you away and he was like a bride left at the church.

Lacey's distress shows it is true. Barbara speaks with sudden and surprising venom

Barbara I do not snatch people away!
Reston Oh yes you do, my darling. You snatch what you want and then throw it away because it was too easy.
Barbara Something that's thrown at one is always too easy.
Reston Something! That's just about your mark, isn't it? But it wasn't just me, was it? It was Jack, then Don, then me. You've been through us all like a child eating sweets. You even had a go at converting Lacey. We've all been Barbara'd at one time or another.
Barbara God how you make me sick! All of you! It's always Barbara, isn't it? Barbara who holds you back, Barbara who slavedrives you, Barbara who won't let you go out and play, Barbara who takes you behind the woodshed and rapes you. There's always got to be some excuse for your own inadequacies. And it's always Barbara, isn't it! God! I've carried you lot like a bunch of parasites for three years and I'm pig-sick of it. Go and find yourself another meal-ticket! I'm amazed to find one of you has the guts to want to kill me!

Barbara exits to the hall, up the stairs, and off L

There is a silence, and during it a sound from the study of a window-sash rising, and a bump

Barnes Wha . . .
Moore Quiet!

Moore gestures for silence and turns off the lights. The study door opens and one photo-flash sears the room. Then Lewis switches the lights back on

Dave is standing in the centre of the room, looking down at the spot where Connie lay. As the lights go on he shouts with alarm and looks around him bewilderedly

Dave Is she—dead?
Moore Is who dead, Ogden?
Dave Barbara—Miss Love.
Moore Why should you think that?
Dave begins to shake uncontrollably

I said why should you think Miss Love is dead?

Dave I'm not saying anything.
Moore Perhaps I'd better introduce myself formally. I'm *Superintendent* Moore of the Metropolitan Police.

Dave looks startled and glances towards the door of the study as if measuring his chances of escape. He says nothing. Moore notices the glance but continues to gaze impassively at Dave

And you are David Ogden of Three, Crescent Court, Farnham Road, Greenford, Middlesex. Now, we'll sit down and talk this out sensibly.

Dave's head comes up in surprise

Now, when you came here earlier you said you'd been sent to take pictures of Miss Love's Christmas party. That was a lie, wasn't it?

The others look surprised

Dave No.
Moore What *did* you come for, Mr Ogden? And what are you doing here now?

Dave makes no reply. Moore picks up the doll and suddenly confronts Dave with it

Moore Perhaps this will refresh your memory.

The effect on Dave is electrifying

Dave No! I didn't do it! That's not mine. I've never seen that before. Let me go!
Lacey Superintendent . . .
Moore Shut up.

Now Dave starts to babble, the words tumbling over one another

Dave It's all because of that business at the College, isn't it? I knew that's what you'd think. That's why I bolted. I haven't done anything like that since that time at the College. I just wanted a picture of her. Like as if she was a friend. That's why I came back. I wanted to find Miss Love and explain.

Moore lets a silence grow before he asks his next question

Moore How could you explain if you thought she was dead?

Dave is stopped in his tracks. He does not reply

Come now, Ogden, that's a fair enough question.
Dave I—I mean the first time.
Moore You mean you've been back here twice?
Dave Yes.
Moore When was the first time?
Dave About an hour ago.

The others all react

It was all in the dark that time too . . . I climbed in . . .

Moore Through the study window?

Dave Yes, it was unlocked. I didn't know where the lights were, so I let off my flash to see. I came into this room, and there was Miss Love, lying on the floor, dressed up like Santa Claus. I let off another flash to see and make sure. And—and then I heard voices shouting and people running on the landing, so I scarpered.

Moore What made you think she was dead?

Dave Well she—she had a stocking tied round her throat. And she—wasn't moving.

Moore changes his style from tough to friendly. Dave responds

Moore Then why did you run away?

Dave 'Cos I thought I'd get the blame.

Moore Why should you get the blame if you were innocent?

Dave Because I've got a bit of form haven't I? It's all you blokes ever think about.

Moore All right. Did you see anyone else in the room?

Dave I had a feeling someone had just closed the shutters.

Moore I see. Now tell me, Dave, why did you climb in through the study window instead of presenting yourself at the front door?

Dave I didn't think I'd be let in after what happened. But I thought if I could just get in and get Miss Love on her own, I could explain.

Moore And just now—why did you come back a second time?

Dave is silent

Was it to look for—this?

He produces Dave's light meter from the desk. Dave looks as if he's about to bolt again

Dave I—I put it down somewhere. To work the flash, that first time. I didn't miss it till later. I knew if they found it they'd think it was me who did it.

Moore (*springing the trap*) Only if you did do it Ogden, and are guilty of murder.

Dave I should have known better than to trust you! You're no better than the rest. Hauling me out of the house. Questions about this, questions about the doll. I've given my Mum and Dad enough worry. I thought if I could just get my gear, I'd be laughing and nobody would get hurt.

Moore (*admiringly*) Well done, Ogden!

Barnes Oh come on, Moore. It rings true.

Moore Barnes, the day I ask to do your job I'll let you do mine. Now then Dave, just one last point. You say you climbed in through the study window, came in here and saw Miss Love lying on the floor, dressed like Santa Claus.

Dave Yeah, that's right.

Moore How did you know it was Miss Love?

Dave is at a loss. He is totally silent

How did you know, Dave?

Dave Well—it was obvious, wasn't it?

Moore It was very far from obvious. She was wearing a Santa Claus outfit and the hood was pulled forward over her face. How did you know it was she? Wouldn't it have been much more likely that it was a man?

Dave I heard her say she was going to dress up.

Moore No, that won't do, Dave. Nothing was said about that until after you'd gone.

Dave Well, I must have . . . read it in a magazine then. That its something she does at Christmas. I've got everything that's ever been written about her, you know. Yeah, that's it—I read it somewhere.

Moore turns to the others

Moore Has anything like that ever been published in a magazine?

They shake their heads

Barnes Not to my knowledge.

Moore goes to the door to the hall, and shouts up the stairs.

Moore Would you mind coming down a minute, please?

A moment later, Barbara enters, on the landing. At sight of her, Dave jumps up involuntarily, looks towards where the body lay. He draws in his breath quickly. Barbara's hand flies to her throat

Dave Barbara!

Moore I'm sorry to trouble you, Miss Love, but it is rather important. Has your little Santa Claus tradition ever been published in the press?

Barbara No—no, I don't think so.

Dave Look, it has!

Moore That's enough, Ogden, get your gear together.

Barbara What did he come back for this time? Is—he . . .?

Moore Let us say he'll be of great help to us in our enquiries.

Barbara Oh but—but I'm not sure about the Santa Claus business. I wouldn't want . . .

Moore Don't let it worry you. There's a great deal more to it than that. I'd like to see the rest of you at the station tomorrow at ten o'clock sharp. You too, please, Miss Love. I'm sure you've nothing more to worry about but I'll send a policewoman along to spend the night here if you wish.

Barbara Yes, please. And—thank you.

Moore My pleasure. Till tomorrow then. Come on, Ogden.

Dave But I *did* read it.

Moore We'll hear all about that down at the station.

Dave and Moore exit

Barbara turns to the others, bewildered about Dave

Barbara How did he—I mean . . .
Reston He came back. For something he dropped when . . .
Barnes Barbara, are you all right? Look, we'll stay with you tonight. We can doss down in here.
Reston No, there's no need for us all to stay. I'll hang on.
Barbara (*coldly*) I'll be perfectly all right. There's no need for anyone to stay.
Lewis But Barbara . . .
Barbara The policewoman will be here soon and at the moment I'd prefer her company to yours.
Lacey If it's about what was said . . .
Barbara I'd simply like to be on my own.

They start to go, ill at ease and shamefaced

Barnes Well, if you're sure . . .
Reston Goodnight, Barbara.
Lewis Goodnight.
Lacey Good night, Barbara, and merry er . . .
Barbara Wait!

They stop

(*bitterly*) You forgot your presents. (*She gets them and hands them out one by one. Then turns her back as if they'd ceased to exist*)

The men all exit, leaving Barbara alone. She goes through the door to the kitchen. We hear cups and a kettle being rattled. She re-enters, closes the study door, then pulls the living-room doors together

There is a creak from the study. Barbara, startled, goes to the bar drawer for the gun. She looks in both bar drawers for bullets, but can't find them. She goes to the desk drawer and takes out a magazine, which she loads into the gun. With great trepidation, she goes to the study, switches on the lights, then throws open the door. Nobody is there. She closes the door, turns off the lights, then puts the gun in the desk drawer

Barbara takes up her glass of brandy and exits to the kitchen

There is the sound of the sash window opening in the study. Then the study door starts to open and a black gloved hand reaches through

Barbara closes the kitchen louvres and the hand retreats, closing the study door. Barbara enters the room, and starts to go to the study, when the kettle whistle blows and she exits back into the kitchen. The study door opens slowly and Moore comes quietly out. He crosses to the bar and starts searching the drawers. He hears Barbara, closes the drawers, and turns round.

Barbara enters with her tea tray, sees Moore, and screams

Moore goes to her to relieve her of the tray

Moore Steady, Barbara, I'll take that.
Barbara God, what a shock you gave me!
Moore I'm sorry, Barbara, it was clumsy of me.
Barbara How on earth did you get in?
Moore Through the study window. It's far too easy. Oh, don't worry. I've locked it now.
Barbara But why come in through the window?
Moore I was afraid he might be here.
Barbara Who?
Moore Young Ogden.
Barbara How could he be here?
Moore He got away from me. Suddenly took off like the Concorde.
Barbara So he could still be prowling about out there.
Moore All the way back I kept hoping you had a gun. Have you got a gun, Barbara?
Barbara No.
Moore You can tell me. I wouldn't pinch you for not having a licence.
Barbara No, I haven't got a gun.
Moore But you're a member of the Chelsea Rifle Club.
Barbara How did you know that?
Moore I know a great deal about you, my dear.
Barbara I leave my gun at the club. When is the policewoman coming?
Moore I forgot to tell you. There wasn't one available. I shall stay with you myself. Do have your tea.
Barbara Would you like some?
Moore That would be nice.
Barbara I'll get you a cup.

Barbara exits to the kitchen

Moore takes the key out of the study door and puts it in the off-stage side of the door. Then he closes the door

Barbara enters with a cup and saucer

Barbara Do you take sugar?
Moore Just a little milk please.

She gives him his tea

Quite the domestic scene.
Barbara Yes, I suppose it is.
Moore Such a pity you're not married, Barbara. You'd make a delicious wife.
Barbara I've had my chances.

Moore Preferred to go on playing the field, eh?
Barbara I've simply concentrated on my career.
Moore Never wanted children?
Barbara Five million little fans are a substitute.
Moore But they can never take the place of the real thing, surely.
Barbara I really don't know, I've never had time to think.
Moore Yes, you've been very single-minded.
Barbara Funny that always sounds good about a man but bad about a woman.
Moore Yes, it does seem unfair. But it gets better as a woman matures.
Barbara In what way?
Moore A career woman of thirty-five is acceptable. A career girl of nineteen is rather repellent.
Barbara I'd say it depends on the woman and on the girl.
Moore Then let's construct a scenario as they say in the White House. Let's suppose that our girl of nineteen has a baby by her boyfriend. And let's say that her boyfriend loved her very much and wanted to marry her. But she didn't want to marry him and she didn't want the baby—because both would interfere with her budding career on television. So she gave the baby away into adoption despite the father's pleas. (*He locks the living room door and pockets the key*)
Barbara What the hell are you doing?
Moore Wouldn't you say that was a hard little madam?
Barbara Give me that key.
Moore Girls like that are so destructive. She ruined that man's life. He never got over losing her—or his child. And as for the child—his parents never told him he was adopted. He found that out for himself. It made him slightly odd. He pesters celebrities to take their photographs—looking for security, I suppose. You recognized your son, very quickly, didn't you?
Barbara I'd been told where he lived, what school he was at, that was all.
Moore And the little finger helped, of course.
Barbara He was born with it. Who are you?

Barbara switches on the tape recorder without his noticing

Moore I'm a scientist, Barbara. Communications systems. (*Imitates Ansaphone voice*) We have all kinds of gadgets. Like the one I tapped into your telephone so that when you dialled the Chelsea Police, you got me.
Barbara (*whispers*) Why?
Moore My brother committed suicide when you left him and took his baby away. He died a tormented man. I swore then I'd watch you die the same way.
Barbara No . . .

Moore picks up the doll and waves it at her. Slowly he draws the stocking from its neck

Moore This is how you'll look, Barbara, Catch!

He throws it at her. She shrieks, making no attempt to catch it. It hits her and drops to the floor. With a little cry, she rushes towards the study, tugs at the handle

Locked, I'm afraid.

She rushes across to the main door and tugs at them

Oh, come on now—you saw me lock that one yourself.

He advances on her, the stocking stretched between his hands. Making a kind of dry sobbing noise, she dodges behind the right chair. Moore is on one side of it, she on the other. They're like children playing tag. As he makes to move around one side, she moves up to the far end. As he moves in the opposite direction, so does she

Just like "Tag", isn't it? Just like "Tag".

Finally Barbara lures him almost around her side then makes a break and runs for the desk. She flings herself at the desk and scrabbles desperately at the drawer with her gun in it. It sticks, she tugs frantically and it opens. But by this time Moore is on her. He whips the stocking around her throat, forces her over the desk

I'm sorry I killed Connie. But there'll be no mistake this time.

Her hands thrash wildly in the drawer of the desk. She finds the gun and pulls herself free, covers him with the gun. There is a pause

Barbara You fool! You bloody fool! You nearly did strangle me!
Moore That was my intention.
Barbara Oh come on, Superintendent, I knew what you were up to from the start.
Moore That was very astute of you.
Barbara All that stuff about being a scientist and my fiancé's brother! You're not a scientist, and my fiancé didn't have a brother! You're a policeman and a pretty desperate one to try a trick like that.
Moore Then you won't be needing the gun, will you.
Barbara Oh no, you're far too dangerous. I warn you, it wouldn't take much to make me pull the trigger at the moment. You thought that if you pretended to be the murderer, you'd get me so confused, I'd give something away. But what, for God's sake? What am I supposed to be hiding?
Moore Oh, your plan was beautifully conceived. It was almost tragic that you slipped up at the last moment.
Barbara I don't know what you're talking about.
Moore Just before I took Ogden away, you came down the stairs and said: "What did he come back for this time?"
Barbara So?
Moore Only the one who did it could have known that he had been back before, because only the one who did it could have seen the flashes from his camera. None of us knew Ogden had been back before until he told

us so himself. And nobody told you. So I realized that you had killed Connie.

Barbara Why on earth should I want to kill Connie?

Moore Yes. That's what I asked myself. So I looked at her diary when I got outside. (*He starts to get it from his pocket*)

Barbara Careful!

Moore She knew that Ogden was your son and why you gave him away.

Barbara I'll take that.

Moore throws it at her, to distract her, but she keeps the gun on him and he sinks back. She picks up diary

Thank you, Superintendent.

Moore She was blackmailing you, wasn't she? She could have blown all this sky-high for you by telling the public that the darling of the kiddies had given away her own baby. She even arranged for the boy to be sent here tonight. She wanted you to recognize him and you did. But what she didn't know was that you'd already planned to get rid of her.

Barbara You seem to forget that it was I who got the threats.

Moore Of course. You sent them all to yourself. You even managed to push the glass. Then you persuaded Connie to take your place as Santa Claus and you strangled her.

Barbara It's all guesswork isn't it. You haven't one shred of real evidence.

Moore I'll get my evidence.

Barbara You won't be getting any more evidence, Superintendent. You're the only one who knows about that diary. And I'm going to kill you.

Moore People don't just kill Police Superintendents and get away with it.

Barbara Ah, but you're not a Police Superintendent, are you? You told me so yourself. You were very convincing. Stay where you are! (*She goes to the tape recorder and winds it back*) Now!

Moore (*on tape*) I'm a scientist, Barbara. Communications systems. We have all kinds of gadgets.

Barbara (*winding on*) Fascinating, isn't it. Now let's see what else we have.

Moore (*on tape*) Just like tag. I'm sorry I killed Connie but there'll be no mistake this time . . . (*Followed by the sound of Barbara being strangled*)

Barbara You see? Nobody in the world could blame me for shooting someone who was strangling me.

Moore What a very ingenious lady you are, Miss Love.

Barbara Yes, I am, rather.

The doorbell rings. They both react. Then the sound of carol singing is heard

Only more carol singers, Superintendent—not the Seventh Cavalry I'm afraid.

The door bell rings again

Now let me see . . . Don't move! I'm bent over the desk, you're choking the life out of me—I scrabble in the drawer, get the gun, stick it into you there, I should say . . .

The doorbell rings again

In my panic I fire three times. Better to be safe than sorry. Pity really—I found you rather exciting. Well now, the carol singers seem to have given up the ghost.

Moore But I haven't. It's all right—you can come out now!

Barbara Oh, come on, Superintendent.

Dave comes through the study door

You bastard! (*She steps back, covering them both*)

Moore You see, I have my evidence. A witness.

Barbara (*looking calculatingly at Dave, then back at Moore*) I don't think he is your witness. I think he's going to be mine. After all, he did hear you try to kill me, and he's my son. (*She stiffens her arm as if to fire*)

Dave No!

Dave jumps forward and knocks down her gun arm. Moore grabs her arm and takes the gun

Moore Shall we go?

Barbara turns to Dave

Barbara You know, it's true what they say—one's children are always a disappointment.

CURTAIN

FURNITURE AND PROPERTY LIST

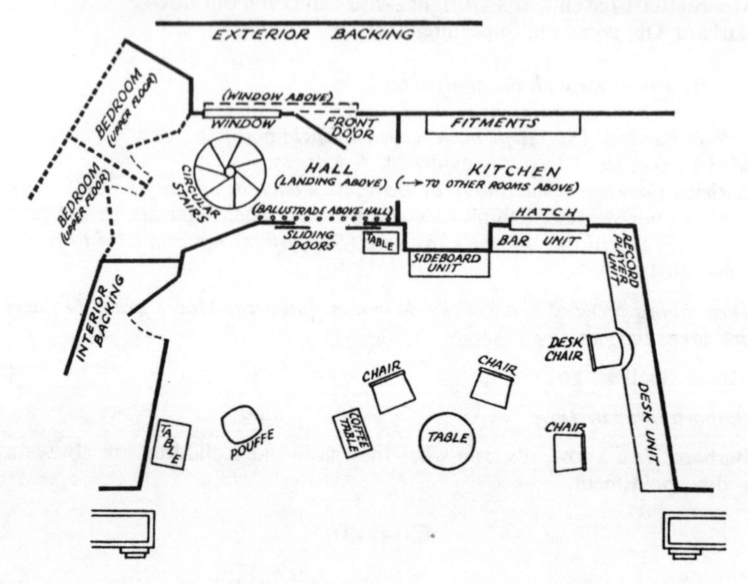

ACT I

Scene 1

On stage: 3 large armchairs
1 large pouffe
1 desk chair
Coffee table. *On it:* ashtray
Low circular table (c) *On it:* ashtray, cigarette box, lighter
Small table (up c) *On it:* tape recorder (practical)
Occasional table (down r) *On it:* ashtray, cigarette box, lighter
Sideboard unit. *On it:* Christmas cards
Bar unit. *On it:* Vodka, gin, scotch, campari, brandy, Glenfiddich, tonic water, soda syphon, water jug, ice bucket, lemon in dish, tea towel and spoon, Ouija tumbler, glass with ice and water, glasses *In drawers:* Lexicon cards in box, gun
Record player unit. *On it:* coffin box with coffin, doll and stocking, Christmas presents, records including "Who" album
Desk unit. *On it:* blotter, writing materials, books, ashtray, Ansaphone (practical), telephone, copy of *Daily Express*. *In drawer:* gun magazine
Television set in wall with sliding picture to cover it
Christmas tree with presents arranged round it
By front door; letters
Carpet
Window curtains

Off stage: Christmas parcels **(Barbara)**
Evening paper with bill **(Connie)**

Personal: **Barbara:** doorkey

SCENE 2

Strike: Coffin and box
Christmas cards and envelopes
Evening paper

Set: Doll on coffee table

Off stage: Christmas presents **(Lewis, Lacey, Reston)**
Champagne bottles **(Connie, Barnes)**

SCENE 3

Off stage: Camera with case and flood lamps **(Dave)**
Nut **(Lewis)**
2 glasses of champagne **(Lacey)**
Nutcrackers and plate of canapés **(Barnes)**
Name cards **(Connie)**

Personal: **Lacey:** Dunhill lighter

ACT II

SCENE 1

Off stage: Paper hats, masks **(Lacey, Lewis, Barnes, Reston)**
Light meter **(Moore)**
Santa Claus mask and cloak **(Barbara)**
Stocking **(Barbara)**

SCENE 2

Strike: Masks, hats

Set: Doll on coffee table
Light meter on desk

Off stage: Tray with teapot, milk jug, sugar bowl, 1 cup, 1 saucer, 1 spoon **(Barbara)**
Cup and saucer **(Barbara)**
Stocking **(Moore)**
Diary **(Moore)**

In kitchen: Dressing as required. Props supposedly brought in from the kitchen may be pre-set there, or off stage as convenient

LIGHTING PLOT

Property fittings required: wall brackets, table lamp, strip lights (kitchen and landing), fairy lights on Christmas tree, television effect
INTERIOR: a living room, kitchen, hall and landing

ACT I SCENE 1. Early evening

To open: Dim exterior lighting. Fairy and television only on

Cue 1 — **Barnes** switches off television (Page 1)
Television off

Cue 2 — **Barnes** switches on lights (Page 1)
Snap on living-room, hall and landing lights

ACT I SCENE 2. Twenty minutes later

To open: As close of Scene 1

Cue 3 — **Barbara** and **Connie** go to kitchen (Page 19)
Snap on kitchen lights

ACT I SCENE 3. One minute later

To open: As close of Scene 2

Cue 4 — **Lacey** switches off lights (Page 33)
Snap off all lighting except Christmas tree

Cue 5 — **Lacey** switches on bracket lamp (Page 33)
Snap on bracket lamp

Cue 6 — **Reston:** "What does that mean?" (Page 35)
Blackout

ACT II SCENE 1. Immediately following

To open: All interior lighting on

Cue 7 — **Connie** switches off lights (Page 42)
Snap out all lighting except tree and bracket

Cue 8 — **Barbara** moves to desk (Page 42)
Blackout

Cue 9 — Shouts from upstairs (Page 42)
Snap on landing light

Cue 10 — **Moore** enters (Page 42)
Snap on remaining lights

ACT II SCENE 2. One hour later

To open: As close of Scene 1

Cue 11 — **Moore** switches off lights (Page 48)
Blackout

Cue 12 — **Lewis** switches on lights (Page 48)
Return to previous lighting

EFFECTS PLOT

ACT I

Scene 1

Cue 1	At Curtain rise *Television programme and music*	(Page 1)
Cue 2	**Barnes** switches off TV set *Programme off*	(Page 1)
Cue 3	**Barnes:** ". . . before they can spell it" *Doorbell rings*	(Page 3)
Cue 4	**Barbara** switches on Ansaphone *Ansaphone on*	(Page 5)
Cue 5	**Barbara** switches on Ansaphone *Ansaphone on*	(Page 8)

Scene 2

Cue 6	**Moore:** ". . . Shall we hear it now?"	(Page 12)
Cue 7	**Moore:** ". . . one of your guests" *Doorbell rings*	(Page 13)
Cue 8	**Barbara:** ". . . are just objects" *Doorbell rings*	(Page 15)
Cue 9	**Barnes:** ". . . purely professional" *Doorbell rings*	(Page 18)
Cue 10	**Moore:** ". . . in Montpelier Square" *Doorbell rings*	(Page 20)
Cue 11	**Moore:** "Shall we go in?" *Doorbell rings*	(Page 22)

Scene 3

Cue 12	**Lacey** puts glass on table *Telephone rings*	(Page 33)
Cue 13	**All:** ". . . Who did that?" *Ansaphone on*	(Page 35)

ACT II

Scene 1

Cue 14	**Connie:** "Will you be all right?" *Telephone rings*	(Page 37)
Cue 15	**Connie** starts tape recorder *Music—"Jingle Bells"*	(Page 42)

Cue 16	**Barbara** moves to desk *Music stops*	(Page 42)
Cue 17	**Barbara**: "No! Please!" *Music restarts at high speed*	(Page 42)
Cue 18	**Barnes** switches off recorder *Music stops*	(Page 43)
Cue 19	**Barbara** exits *Sound of window sash, and a bump*	(Page 48)
Cue 20	**Barbara** exits to kitchen *Sound of window sash*	(Page 52)
Cue 21	**Barbara** moves towards study *Kettle whistles*	(Page 52)
Cue 22	**Barbara**: ". . . Stay where you are!" *Tape recorder on*	(Page 56)
Cue 23	**Barbara**: "Yes, I am, rather" *Doorbell rings, followed by carol singers*	(Page 56)
Cue 24	**Barbara**: ". . . the Seventh Cavalry, I'm afraid" *Doorbell rings*	(Page 56)
Cue 25	**Barbara**: "I should say" *Doorbell rings*	(Page 56)